CITYSPOTS

SARAJEVO

WHAT'S IN YOUR GUIDEBOOK?

Independent authors Impartial up-to-date information from our travel experts who meticulously source local knowledge.

Experience Thomas Cook's 165 years in the travel industry and guidebook publishing enriches every word with expertise you can trust.

Travel know-how Thomas Cook has thousands of staff working around the globe, all living and breathing travel.

Editors Travel-publishing professionals, pulling everything together to craft a perfect blend of words, pictures, maps and design.

You, the traveller We deliver a practical, no-nonsense approach to information, geared to how you really use it.

CITYSPOTS

SARAJEVO

Written by Tim Clancy
Updated by Dino Zulumovic

Published by Thomas Cook Publishing
A division of Thomas Cook Tour Operations Limited
Company registration No: 3772199 England
The Thomas Cook Business Park, 9 Coningsby Road
Peterborough PE3 8SB, United Kingdom
Email: books@thomascook.com, Tel: +44 (0)1733 416477
www.thomascookpublishing.com

Produced by The Content Works Ltd
Aston Court, Kingsmead Business Park, Frederick Place
High Wycombe, Bucks HP11 1LA
www.thecontentworks.com

Series design based on an original concept by Studio 183 Limited

ISBN: 978-1-84848-137-4

Series Editor: Lucy Armstrong
Production/DTP: Steven Collins

Printed and bound in Spain by GraphyCems

CONTENTS

INTRODUCING SARAJEVO

MAKING THE MOST OF SARAJEVO

THE CITY OF SARAJEVO

OUT OF TOWN TRIPS

PRACTICAL INFORMATION

MAPS

SYMBOLS KEY

The following symbols are used throughout this book:

address telephone website address email
opening times public transport connections important

The following symbols are used on the maps:

information office
airport
hospital
police station
bus station
railway station
cathedral
points of interest
city
large town
small town
main road
minor road
railway
numbers denote featured cafés & restaurants

Hotels and restaurants are graded by approximate price as follows:
£ budget price **££** mid-range price **£££** expensive

The Sarajevo Clock Tower dominates the horizon

INTRODUCING
Sarajevo

Introduction

The long valley of the River Miljacka runs a direct east–west route before flowing into the River Bosna. It is here, in this gorgeous mountain valley, that the city of Sarajevo, today's capital of Bosnia and Herzegovina, was built. Sarajevo's geographical position can be viewed as sheer coincidence, but its role as the hub should not be underestimated.

Walking through Sarajevo is equivalent to walking along an historical timeline. The quaint old Turkish quarter of Baščaršija, built in the 15th and 16th centuries, has retained its authentic characteristics as a buzzing oriental trading centre. The Austro-Hungarian era city centre very much resembles old Vienna, with its trademark architecture and superb urban spacing. This is followed by the occasionally daunting socialist architecture of Tito's era, when the city expanded fivefold in as many decades.

Sarajevo is not a city of majestic museums or perfectly preserved medieval castles. It is a fun and vibrant city with a uniquely effervescent café culture. It has been coined the fastest-changing city in Europe – the reasons being fairly obvious. The city was brought to its knees during the longest siege in modern European history, from 1992–5; Sarajevo has re-emerged though and, in fact, has been transformed from a provincial capital to a bustling and exciting European capital city.

Sarajevo is indeed a beautiful city, endowed with the influences of many cultures from both East and West, but it is truly the people that make the place, a place that will quickly

feel like home. As a capital city, it has many of the advantages of a metropolis, but also maintains a small-town, welcoming and safe feel. It's compact, and fairly easy to navigate, especially on foot, with a friendly face on nearly every corner.

Old nišan *(Muslim gravestone) overlooking the city*

When to go

Sarajevo is a classic, four-season tourist destination, with a plethora of delights to entrance the visitor at any time of the year.

SEASONS & CLIMATE

Sarajevo enjoys a classic alpine continental climate. Summer is certainly the high season, with the largest number of guests and the warmest temperatures. From June to mid-September visitors can count on rather warm, and often quite hot, conditions. July and August temperatures can reach up to 40°C (104°F) but the mountains usually keep things cool in the evenings.

The city is aglow with the colours of spring by late April and early May: the latter month is a truly beautiful time to visit the city. The long winter thaw is over in the low Miljacka Valley and Sarajevans, so anxious to re-embrace their love for outdoor cafés, are just waiting for the first signs of warmer weather to peel off the layers of winter clothes and bask in the sun over a coffee and a cigarette.

Come autumn time the city clings to every sunny day – keeping the outdoor cafés open well into November. October is known for its *babino ljeto* (grandmother's summer), which often produces perfect sunny days – with temperatures ranging from 14–20°C (57–68°F) during the day but cool in the evening, dipping into single digits.

Sarajevo can get its first snows in November but the ski season doesn't usually open up until December, often mid-month. Catholic Christmas, New Year, Orthodox Christmas and Orthodox New Year all add to the festive ski season mode.

Jahorina and Bjelašnica, in the Olympic Mountains, are hotspots in late December, all of January and early February.

ANNUAL EVENTS

February & March

Sarajevska Zima (Sarajevo Winter) From mid-February to the end of March, Sarajevo hosts a regional theatre festival of

The Bosnian lily flowers in parks and gardens in late spring

friendship with colleagues from former Yugoslavia. ⓐ Titova 9A ⓣ 033 207 945 ⓦ www.sarajevskazima.ba

July

Baščaršijske Noći (Baščaršija Nights) This month-long, completely free celebration is a great event at the height of the tourist season. Sarajevo in July is always teeming with visitors, and the Baščaršija Nights features entertainment ranging from art exhibitions to outdoor concerts and contemporary dance performances. JU Sarajevo Art/Sarajevo Arts Agency ⓐ Dalmatinska 2/1 ⓣ 033 207 921, 207 929 ⓦ www.bascarsijskenoci.ba

Internacionalni Folklorni Festival (International Folklore Festival) Although the festival does attract some western nations, the highlight is most certainly the strong tradition of folk music and dance from eastern Europe. JU Sarajevo Art/ Sarajevo Arts Agency ⓐ Dalmatinska 2/1 ⓣ 033 207 921, 207 929 ⓦ www.sarajevoarts.ba/festivalfolklora_eng.html

August

Sarajevo Film Festival End of August. This has become the most popular film festival in southeastern Europe. It's a laid-back affair showing a wide range of films, with special competitions for regional films, documentaries and features highlighting human rights. ⓐ Zelenih beretki 12/1, Obala Art Centar Hamdije Kreševljakovića 13 ⓣ 033 221 516, 209 411 ⓦ www.sff.ba

September

Teatar Fest This festival allows artists from all over the region to take the stage. Even though there are no translations of the plays, it is still a unique experience to witness. Many of the performances are free of charge. a Pruščakova 12/1 t 033 442 958 w www.tf.com.ba

October

MESS End of October. This alternative theatre festival is the country's longest running theatrical event. The festival is expanding year on year and has attracted some of the world's best alternative theatres to take part. a Maršala Tita 54/1 t 033 200 392 w www.mess.ba

November

Jazz Fest First week in November. The Jazz Fest is becoming known as a venue for small and intimate shows with big name jazz artists, as well as free jam sessions in jazz clubs around town after the show. Tickets can be purchased online and there is good information about all the acts. t 033 550 480 w www.jazzfest.ba

PUBLIC HOLIDAYS

Nova Godina (Catholic New Year) 1 Jan
Pravoslavni Božić (Orthodox Christmas) 7 Jan
Pravoslavna Nova godina (Orthodox New Year) 14 Jan
Dan Nezavisnosti (Independence Day) 1 Mar
Praznik Rada (Labour Day) 1 May
Katolički Božić (Catholic Christmas) 25 Dec
Bajram (Muslim Holy Day) This date is related to moon cycles and differs each year

Sarajevo Film Festival

What many people don't know about the siege of Sarajevo was the art of resistance that not only kept Sarajevo alive, but also defined Sarajevo's post-war cultural scene. Few are aware of the war theatre that gave performances in the basement of the National Theatre throughout the conflict, or the fact that one of Europe's top ten film festivals was a creation of this artistic, anti-war resistance. The Sarajevo Film Festival (SFF) is a war baby, born in 1995 during the last year of the hostilities.

The idea of Mirsad Purivatra, a professor at Sarajevo's film academy, the Festival was designed to continue to defy the siege through artistic means and provide some sort of 'normality' to a life that was anything but normal. Films and some of their directors were brought through the 700 m (2,296 ft) tunnel under Sarajevo Airport – and with the help of friends, family and a bit of luck, the first Sarajevo Film Festival was a success.

Over ten years later it is now one of Europe's premiere film festivals and the largest festival in southeast Europe. Filmmakers and film lovers from both East and West flock to Sarajevo in August for the event, which has a strong focus on regional films and international documentaries. A vast range of famous artists such as Nick Nolte, John Malkovich, Mike Leigh, Gérard Depardieu and Carole Bouquet have visited and participated in the festival.

What makes the Sarajevo Film Festival particularly special is the absence of paparazzi and the lack of distance between the fans and the stars. It is a laid-back occasion with many opportunities for the public to meet and speak with filmmakers and their casts. Tickets are accessible to everyone and the SFF make sure that they are always available at the festival itself. You can buy tickets pre-sale by phone, at the box office during the festival and just before the movie starts for an amazingly affordable price (see page 12 for details).

Billboards for the Sarajevo Film Festival line the River Miljacka

History

Due to its unique location in the heart of the Balkan peninsula, Sarajevo has acted as a gateway of peoples and empires from Asia Minor and Europe since ancient times. Although Sarajevo had been a settlement since at least the early Neolithic era, it only became a city in the middle of the 15th century with the great efforts of the Ottoman Empire. Life in Sarajevo under the Ottomans, from both an economic and cultural point of view, developed at an increasingly rapid pace during the 16th and 17th centuries, and although under Ottoman rule, there was a relatively equal balance of its Christian and Muslim populations for most of that time. A small Sephardic Jewish community was introduced in the early 16th century after being expelled from Spain. Even back then, Sarajevo was a unique multi-ethnic and multiconfessional city.

After the collapse of the Ottoman empire in 1878, Sarajevo for the first time experienced a European cultural renaissance. European-structured schools and research institutes were opened and Sarajevo's young intellectuals were educated in Vienna and Budapest. The first railway was also built. Alongside these developments, however, was also growing social resistance to another occupying force in Sarajevo – the Austro-Hungarian Empire.

This came to a head on 28 June 1914 when a young Serbian nationalist, Gavrilo Princip, assassinated Archduke Franz Ferdinand, the Austro-Hungarian heir, and his pregnant wife Sofia on the Latinska Ćuprija (Latin Bridge) (see page 68). It was this event that ignited World War I.

Later, after the World War II victory by the anti-fascist resistance movement, Tito's Partisans, Sarajevo developed rapidly.

The population grew considerably and the territory expanded to include ten new municipalities. The highlight of Sarajevo's socialist revolution under Tito was the 1984 Winter Olympics, which was, at the time, the largest Winter Olympic Games in history.

The war that ravaged Sarajevo for over 1,400 days from 1992–5 was the longest siege in modern European history. Over 11,000 people were killed, including 1,500 children, while under UN protection. Yet, Sarajevans of all ethnic backgrounds still celebrate their diversity and identify themselves as European. It is this spirit of resistance and diversity that still characterises the city.

Sarajevo has emerged from the ashes as a thriving and fast-growing capital city. Many of its national and cultural monuments have been rebuilt, and it is once again the centre of political, cultural and spiritual life in Bosnia and Herzegovina.

Latinska Ćuprija (Latin Bridge), where Franz Ferdinand was assassinated

Lifestyle

Even though Sarajevo is a capital city, and one of the fastest growing cities in Europe, the pace of life is considerably slower than in most European capitals. People are dedicated to friends and family and find time for socialising and social events. Two key phrases help visitors understand the lifestyle of the average Sarajevan – *sabur*, meaning 'take it slow', and *bujrum*, meaning 'you are most welcome'.

Social life, business deals, dating, or catching up with friends all revolve around one key factor – coffee. And there are enough cafés in town to prove it. The café culture is very dominant among all age groups; whether it be hip and modern cafés or sitting in the garden with family, coffee is in many ways the vice that defines the Bosnian social fabric.

Even though the average worker in Sarajevo earns less than €350 per month, they are extremely generous people when it comes to friends, food and drink. It is very common for people to ask others for a coffee or a drink. The general rule is that the one who offered the invite covers the bill. It may be considered rude to try and pay just for your drink and not the other.

Many of the cafés in Sarajevo are owned by the Islamic community, particularly in the old quarters. These establishments do not sell alcohol. It is not possible to tell which places are owned by the Islamic community but it is not considered offensive to ask for alcohol in a place that doesn't serve it.

Sarajevans, and indeed most Bosnians, are intense meat lovers. There are two pastimes designed for the enjoyment of fine Bosnian meat: *meze*, which is the slow consumption of alcohol and usually dry meat and cheese; and *roštilj* (barbecue). Sarajevans are not shy about their love for grilled meat, especially lamb and *ćevapi* (small meat sausages).

Sarajevo has a majority Muslim population with a smaller Orthodox and Catholic group and a minute Jewish community. All communities are largely secular and well integrated. If entering a home in Sarajevo, it is tradition to take off your shoes, regardless of your religion.

In summer the cafés spill onto the streets

Culture

Sarajevo's cultural life is markedly weighed in terms of 'before and after' the war, with contemporary art, in all its forms, very much shaped by the events of the 1992–5 siege. Here is a small summary of the city's thriving art world.

The Narodno Pozorište (National Theatre) has been in existence since 1921 and somehow managed to stage theatre productions even through the worst periods of the war. Today the theatre is as active as ever with plays and concerts showing most of the year. It is also the main venue for the Sarajevo Film Festival in late August (see page 12).

Sarajevo has always been well known in the former Yugoslavia for its brilliant filmmakers; this tradition is alive and well with hit films coming out every year. Examples include the Oscar-winning film *No-Man's Land* by Danis Tanović and Jasmila Žbanić's film *Grbavica*, which took the Golden Bear at the 2006 Berlin Film Festival and was nominated for an Oscar. Countless other high-quality movies include *Savršeni Krug* (Perfect Circle) by Ademir Kenović, *Gori Vatra* (Fuse) by Pjer Žalica, *Remake* by Dino Mustafić and *Ljeto u Zlatnoj Dolini* (Summer in the Golden Valley), the 2004 winner of the Rotterdam Film Festival Tiger award. Namik Kabil's film *Kod Amidže Idri* (Days and Hours) is a fantastic depiction of the subtleties and sometimes peculiar relations of an average Sarajevan family.

The greatest writers in Sarajevo's history emerged in post-World War II socialist Yugoslavia. Ivo Andrić, Bosnia's only Nobel Laureate, continued his literary domination with *Na Drini Ćuprija* (Bridge over the Drina) and *Travnička Hronika* (Travnik Chronicle).

Mid-performance at the Narodno Pozorište (National Theatre)

Although he was born in Travnik, he spent many of his school years in Sarajevo. In the most recent post-war era Sarajevo has produced literary thinkers like Aleksandar Hemon, Nenad Veličković, Faruk Šehić, Dario Džamonja, Dževad Karahasan and Marko Vešović. Philosopher and writer Ivan Lovrenović offers one of the most insightful and objective viewpoints into Bosnia's cultural history. The works of many of the writers mentioned here have been translated into English.

Sarajevo is also the centre of Bosnia and Herzegovina's modern music scene. The tradition of rock and alternative music has never died, and groups like Skroz, Letu Štuke, Sikter and Dubioza Kolektiv still attract big crowds and play at venues throughout the country.

Many Sarajevans pride themselves on sophisticated cultural taste, including an appreciation for high-quality classical music. Musicians have been a crucial part of the restoration of Sarajevo, giving voice to suffering and offering healing through their notes. Three institutions are prominent in Sarajevo's classical music scene: Narodno Pozorište (National Theatre), with its Philharmonic Orchestra, Opera and Ballet; Muzička Akademija Univerziteta u Sarajevu (Music Academy of Sarajevo University); and JU Sarajevo Art, which co-ordinates performances by artists from Bosnia and Herzegovina and beyond.

Sebilj Fountain, Baščaršija (old town)

MAKING THE MOST OF Sarajevo

Shopping

The Sarajevo shopping scene really comes into its own (and becomes truly unique) with the handicraft shops in the old town. These are the workshops – though such a prosaic term seems somehow inadequate to describe venues where real works of art are produced – of *stari zanati* (old handicraftsmen), a term that is very apt when you consider that some of the shops came into being with the arrival of the Ottomans in the mid-15th century. As the city expanded into a major trading centre in Bosnia, so did its volume of trade with faraway lands. As its centre of trade developed, certain streets became

associated with particular arts and crafts, such as 'blacksmith' streets and 'goldsmith' streets. The evolution of these distinct areas continued and in time each craft was located in a particular part of town, as can still be seen today in such places as Kazazi, a street named after the silk tailors, Kazandžiluk, named after the coppersmiths, and Mudželeti, named after the bookbinders. The old town in particular is lined with the shops of *stari zanati* and is worth investigating for economic as well as sociological reasons. Prices for handmade goods are reasonable and local vendors, or *zanatlije*, can be bargained with (though their attitude can be a case of come and have a go if you think you're hard

Pick up some traditional handicrafts in Baščaršija

USEFUL SHOPPING PHRASES

How much is this?
Koliko je ovo?
Koleeko yeh ovo?

That's too expensive
To je preskupo
Too yeh prez-coo-po

Do you have this in my size?
Da li imate ovo u mojoj veličini?
Da lee imat-ee ovo oo moyoy vel-icyee-nee?

OK, I'll take it
Uredu, uzeću
Oo-reh-doo, ooz-eszcoo

enough). Additionally Gazi Husrev-Begov bezistan, located on Ferhadija, is a lovely market with dozens of small shops. This was the centre for silk trade from Asia Minor during Ottoman times.

The classic gift or souvenir from Sarajevo, however, would have to be from Kazandžiluk street. The coppersmiths make fantastic coffee and tea sets that have become trademarks of Sarajevo's handicraftsmen. Be sure to seek out authentic Bosnian-made goods and not the factory-made Turkish souvenirs. You may also find handmade shoes and slippers, high-quality and reasonably priced gold, silver and Bosnian and Persian carpets in the old town.

Modern shops are found mainly on the upper end of Ferhadija, in the Austro-Hungarian city centre area, but also in Maršala Tita and at the Skenderija shopping centre there are Western brand-name stores. Expect to pay similar prices at these outlets as you would in Western Europe.

Eating & drinking

Bosnian cuisine is by no means sophisticated; dishes are rather simple and the spices used are fairly limited. Like most southern European traditions, though, Bosnians take their food seriously, and most visitors rave about the great taste and high quality of local food. There is a large selection of inexpensive but good traditional and international restaurants in Sarajevo. Meats and dairy products are largely organic and the mix of Mediterranean and alpine climates provides a rich array of fruit and vegetables, which are available at markets and served up in restaurants.

There are three main influences in traditional Bosnian cooking: the oriental flavour of Istanbul; Viennese-style meat preparation; and the simple but rather tasty recipes from the rural areas. Many dishes are prepared *Ispod sača* – similar to a Dutch oven: a metal dish is placed on hot coals, the food is placed in the dish and covered by a lid which is then completely covered in hot coals and left to bake. Meat dishes and all types of pita are often cooked in this way.

Pita is the poor man's food, but indeed a tasty one. It comes in many forms and can be found in shops called *buregdžinica*.

PRICE CATEGORIES

The price ratings given in this book indicate the approximate cost of a three-course meal for one person, excluding drinks.

£ up to 8 KM **££** 8–20 KM **£££** over 20 KM

Other local offerings include *burek*, a meat pie; *zeljanica*, which is made from spinach and cheese; *sirnica*, made from a fresh, home-made cheese; and *krompiruša*, a filo-dough with diced potatoes and spices. For a delicious accompaniment to your pita, ask to have *pavlaka*, a fresh cream, or plain yoghurt spread on top.

Breakfast is not that popular in Bosnia so you will have a difficult time finding a 'proper' English breakfast, for example. Lunch is often *ćevapi*, a small, spicy sausage speciality, or pita. Tipping is normal in restaurants but not so much in *ćevabdžinicas* (*ćevapi* places) or *buregdžinicas* (pita places). Ten per cent or less is the norm in most restaurants. In cafés and bars it's normal to

Kod Bibana, a restaurant with a view *(see page 75)*

tip between 1 and 2 KM, depending on the size of your order. ⓘ Be forewarned that most people in Sarajevo smoke and that only a few non-smoking restaurants exist.

LOCAL LIP-SMACKERS

The following is a list of some of the most popular traditional meals:

bamija – okra with veal

begova orba – a very tasty soup, made of chicken and vegetables

bosanski lonac – meat and vegetable stew cooked over an open fire

ćevapi – small meat sausages of lamb and beef mix. They are usually served with fresh onions and pita bread on the side

filovane paprike – fried peppers stuffed with minced meat and spices

jagnjetina – lamb grilled over an open fire

musaka – a meat pie made of minced beef, very similar to shepherd's pie

sarme – meat and rice rolled in cabbage or grape leaves

sitni ćevapi – small chunks of beef in a savoury vegetable sauce

sogandolma – fried onions stuffed with minced meat

teletina – veal, usually served in cutlets. (Veal in Bosnia and Herzegovina is not produced by locking calves in a cage to ensure softer meat.)

USEFUL DINING PHRASES

I'd like a table for (two), please
Molim vas, sto za (dvije) osobe
Moh-leem vas, stow zah (dvey-ye) osobeh

Could I have the bill please?
Račun, molim?
Rachoon, moh-leem?

Excuse me, waiter!
Oprostite, konobar!
Opros-tee-te, ko-no-bar!

I'm a vegetarian
Ja sam vegetarijanac
Jah sam veygee-tar-eeyan-ak

Where is the toilet?
Gdje je toalet?
Gdyeh yeh towalet?

Alcohol is served in most restaurants but never in pita or *ćevapi* places. Local beer is cheap. A half-litre bottle costs around 1 KM in the shops and only 2 or 3 KM in restaurants and bars. Try Sarajevsko, it's the best local beer in the country and, of course, a favourite in Sarajevo. Ožujsko is a good Croatian beer that is also produced locally. Imports are available everywhere. The wine selection will be largely regional. Vranac from Montenegro and Dingač from Croatia, Stankela, Gangaš and Andrija make good local reds, and *Ž*ilavka is a good white grape from Herzegovina. In the shops, a bottle of wine will cost around 5–20 KM and 15–35 KM in restaurants. Local spirits are extremely popular at all times of the day. Made from plums, pears, apples or grapes, the local *rakija* is a very strong brandy.

Entertainment & nightlife

The café culture expands well beyond an afternoon break in Sarajevo: during most of the year, cafés often open until 23.00 or beyond. Many of the relaxing outdoor cafés transform into bars in the evening, with modern music, live DJs and even concerts. Bars are much more popular than discos and clubs, with only a few places that are equivalent to a disco.

For late-night dancing there is the **Boemi Club** (ⓐ Valtera Perića 16 ⓣ 061 374 350) in Marijin Dvor, while **Club FisKultura** (ⓐ Musala B.B. ⓣ 033 184 321 ⓦ www.bock.ba) has live concerts, DJs and late-night music and dancing.

The bar scene is far more developed with great bars throughout the whole city. Most are located within the old town or the city centre (see pages 77 & 94). Highly recommended is a wander around the side streets off Ferhadija in the city centre as well as Zelenih Beretki in the old town, which later turns into Branilaca Sarajeva. This street runs parallel to Ferhadija towards the river, and is home to at least half a dozen of Sarajevo's best bars.

July in Sarajevo has evening events every night with the Baščaršija Nights festival. For film lovers there are a few cinemas in town that regularly screen films with English subtitles or English-speaking films that are subtitled in the local language. There is no dubbing here like in many European countries. **Kino Obala** (ⓐ Hamdije Kreševljakovića 13 ⓣ 033 668 186, 668 187) on the south bank of the River Miljacka is the most modern and comfortable cinema in the city. **Apolo** (ⓐ Mis Irbina 2 ⓣ 033 445 201) behind the presidency is an old-school cinema but with comfy seats. The newest cinema in town is in the **Unitic Twin Towers**

The Victor Bailey group at the Sarajevo Jazz Fest (see page 13)

(ⓐ Fra Anđela Zvizdovića 1 ⓣ 033 295 031). It's a small but modern facility though some have complained about the sound quality. Going to the cinema in Sarajevo is a great bargain, most films cost between 4 and 6 KM. Tickets have to be purchased at the cinema; there is no central ticket office.

The **Narodno Pozorište** (National Theatre ⓐ Obala Kulina Bana 9 ⓣ 033 663 647 ⓔ npsa@bih.net.ba) stages productions most of the year but these are almost exclusively in Bosnian. It is an interesting opportunity, however, to see a version of *Hamlet* set in Ottoman Istanbul, for example. **Kamerni Teatar 55** (Chamber Theatre 55 ⓐ Maršala Tita 56/II ⓣ 033 214 633, 209 041 ⓦ www.kamerniteatar55.ba) is hands-down the best place to see local theatre productions. Many of Sarajevo's best actors are members of this small but very active theatre house. It is located on Maršala Tita near the Eternal Flame. Tickets are sold at the venue.

Street performances are rather rare in Sarajevo. The occasional foreigner may play some music or juggle fire, but, for the most part, entertainment and nightlife in Sarajevo take place indoors. With the exception of Baščaršija Nights, there is also no tradition of open-air concerts – this may change in the near future as many tourists seek concerts, folk dances and outdoor evening entertainment. It is worth knowing that the tourism information centre (see page 136) distributes a free monthly event calendar with all the concerts, operas, events, exhibitions and festivals happening in the city. These are printed in English as well as in the local language.

A spontaneous performance of Bosnian folk music

Sport & relaxation

SPECTATOR SPORTS

As in any European city, football is the god of all sports here. Sarajevo has two clubs: Željo and Sarajevo. A Derby match between the two is certainly something to see. Željo's home terrain is the stadium in Grbavica (Zagrebačka). Sarajevo's home turf is the **Stadion** (Patriotske Lige) where the opening ceremonies of the Olympics were held. Tickets for both are sold beforehand at the two stadiums.

Basketball comes a distant second to football but is nonetheless a well-loved sport in the city. Bosna is the local club and they play in the premier league. All games are played in the Delibašić Arena at the **Skenderija Centre** (Terezija bb www.skenderija.ba), in the centre of town.

PARTICIPATION SPORTS

Walking and hiking the surrounding mountains that flank Sarajevo is definitely one of the best ways to get some exercise and to catch a few unforgettable views of the city and the highland villages. **Green Visions** (Radnička bb 033 717 290, 061 213 278 www.greenvisions.ba) is Sarajevo's only ecotourism group, organising daily hikes around Sarajevo from April to October. Transport, guides and lunch are all provided.

For winter guests there are, of course, the Olympic ski mountains of Jahorina and Bjelašnica. These were the locations for the 14th Winter Olympic Games and they offer the best and most affordable skiing in southeast Europe. Think Olympic-quality skiing for just a fraction of the cost of Western European ski centres.

Ilidža is an ideal place for a walk down Aleja, a 2 km (1 mile) walking and jogging area around the Vrelo Bosne Park. Trams run all day and night from the centre of town to Ilidža.

Ciklo Centar (ⓐ Hamze Čelenke 58, Ilidža ⓣ 033 625 243 ⓦ www.ciklocentar.com) near the park rents bicycles for the day. They also organise mountain biking trips in the mountains.

Preparing to ski in the mountains above Sarajevo

Accommodation

Sarajevo offers a growing range of accommodation throughout the entire city. The number of hotels and *pansions* increases each year. Most accommodation comes in the form of smaller hotels and motels but there is limited capacity, so it is always wise to make reservations in advance, if possible, during the high season, by phone or email. Very few places offer online reservations, and the smaller *pansions* or B&Bs rarely accept credit card payment. The medium and larger sized hotels all accept credit cards.

Most of the accommodation located within the old town and the city centre is ideally situated for getting around everywhere on foot. Some places are up on the hill and require a bit of a trek, but with taxis being reasonably priced, it's not a hassle to hail a cab for the ride back up. If you are looking for peace and quiet then Ilidža is a nice option, with large parks and a much more spacious urban layout. The tram runs dozens of times daily to and from Ilidža: the ride is approximately 30 minutes straight down the valley to the old town.

At the bus and railway stations (conveniently located at the same place) there may be individuals offering private

PRICE CATEGORIES

Gradings used in this book are based on cost per person for two people sharing the least expensive double room with ensuite bathroom and breakfast.

£ up to 50 KM **££** 50–150 KM **£££** over 150 KM

accommodation. Although some may be legitimate, for budget travellers seeking inexpensive private rooms, it's best to go downtown and check out the Ljubičica or Sartour hostels (see page 41). The tramway runs directly from the station to the city centre and the old town all day, every day.

HOTELS

Ada ££ A new hotel situated right in the centre of the old town. This former embassy residency has been converted to a lovely, small hotel with beautiful décor and good service. ⓐ Abdeshana 8

The Ada hotel is a former embassy residence

(The Old Town) 033 475 870, 537 145 www.adahotel.ba Tram: 1, 2, 3, 5

Astra ££ At the upper end of Sarajevo's downtown hotels. The rooms and facilities are very good and not too stark. Zelenih Beretki 9 (The Old Town) 033 252 100, 252 200 www.hotel-astra.com.ba Tram: 1, 2, 3, 5

Hecco ££ Just a short, ten-minute walk from the heart of the old town. This small but attractive hotel offers friendly service, more spacious rooms than normally found in Sarajevo, and wireless internet in all the rooms. Medrese 1 (The Old Town) 033 273 730 www.hotel-hecco.net Tram: 1, 2, 3, 5

Hotel Terme ££ This hotel has recently had a significant facelift, with new rooms and spa facilities added. Terme is a great base for skiing on Bjelašnica or relaxing in Ilidža's green zone outside the busy city centre. Hrasnička cesta 14 (Ilidža) 033 772 100 www.hoteliiilidza.ba Tram: direction Baščaršija–Ilidža

Vila Orient ££ In a superb location in the heart of the old town. Conveniently situated on a quiet sidestreet near Sebilj Fountain, it's a good bargain for a medium-range hotel room. Oprkanj 6 (The Old Town) 033 232 702 www.hotel-vila-orient.com Tram: 1, 2, 3, 5

Holiday Inn £££ This privatised hotel was the famous hotel where journalists camped out during the siege of Sarajevo. It offers the same quality services and facilities as other

The Hecco hotel offers good value

Holiday Inns worldwide. ⓐ Zmaja od Bosne 4 (The Old Town) ⓣ 033 288 000 ⓦ www.holiday-inn.com/sarajevo Tram: direction Baščaršija–Ilidža

Radon Plaza £££ A new, very chic, 5-star hotel at the far end of town between the city centre and Ilidža – the Radon Plaza is in fact the only 5-star hotel in Sarajevo. It has fantastic rooms, a top-floor rotating restaurant, and all the services expected of a top-class hotel. ⓐ Džemala Bijedića 185 (The Old Town/ Ilidža) ⓣ 033 752 900 ⓦ www.radonplazahotel.ba Tram: 2, 3, 5 towards Avaz Business Centre (Stup)

B&Bs

B&B Baščaršija £ Certainly one of the nicest family-owned B&Bs in the city. The service is super-friendly and the rooms reasonable and very clean. Veliki Ćurčiluk 41 (The Old Town) 033 232 185, 061 177 952 heartofthebascarsija@hotmail.com Tram: 1, 2, 3, 5

B&B Lion £ This B&B is in the dead-centre of the old town, in a quiet courtyard just 50 m (55 yds) from the main square. The facilities are new and quite nice and they provide a wide range of services. Bravadžiluk 30 (The Old Town) 033 236 137, 061 268 150 www.lion.co.ba Tram: 1, 2, 3, 5

HOSTELS

Ljubičica £ The city's largest hostel. Most of the accommodation is in private flats, which offer a wide range of services including internet, safety deposit box, laundry and daily tours around and out of town. Mula Mustafe Bašeskije 65 (The Old Town) 033 535 829 www.hostelljubicica.net Tram: 1, 2, 3, 5

Sartour £ One of two hostels in the old town, offering 2–4-person twin-bed accommodation. Breakfast is not included in the price but there is a kitchen at the facilities. Mula Mustafe Bašeskije 63/3 (The Old Town) 061 800 263 www.sartour-hostel-sarajevo.ba Tram: 1, 2, 3, 5 No credit cards

CAMPSITES

Campsite Oaza £ Located in Ilidža, about 30 minutes from the city centre. A full range of facilities for camping includes lots for camper vans, tents and basic bungalow accommodation. Četvrte Viteške Brigade (Ilidža) 033 636 142 www.hoteliilidza.ba Tram: 3, 5 direction Baščaršija–Ilidža

THE BEST OF SARAJEVO

TOP 10 ATTRACTIONS

- **Baščaršija (old town)** The Baščaršija part of the old town of Sarajevo has been a trading centre since the 15th century (see page 64)
- **Ferhadija** This main pedestrian walkway is literally a walk through Sarajevo's history and is teeming with cafés and modern shops (see page 79)
- **Festivals** The *Sarajevo Film Festival* is among the best in Europe. *Baščaršija Nights* last the entire month of July. *The Jazz Fest* in November has a great repertoire of world jazz and *MESS* is the oldest alternative theatre festival in southeast Europe (see page 11)
- **Lukomir Medieval Village** Take an ecotrip and experience one of Europe's last medieval highland villages (see page 115)
- **Vrelo Bosne Park (River Bosna Springs)** The source of the River Bosna in Ilidža is a park overflowing with freshwater springs (see page 102)

- **Historijski Muzej (History Museum)** This tiny museum located in Sarajevo's city centre is the perfect place to get a feel for the history of the place (see page 85)

- ***Ćevapi* and pita** *Ćevapi* are small, tasty, and inexpensive spicy sausages served with pita bread. The pita filo-dough pastries come in many forms: cheese, beef, spinach and potato (see page 27)

- **Tunnel Museum** A tribute to the only self-sustaining lifeline the city of 500,000 people had for over 1,400 days during the war (see page 102)

- **Svrzina Kuća (Svrzo's House)** This is perhaps one of the best-preserved Ottoman homes in the country, so catch a glimpse of how a wealthy family lived in the 18th century (see page 70)

- **Sarajevska Pivara (Sarajevo Brewery)** The brewery has the blessing of not only making good beer but being built on top of a water source (see page 69)

The main Post Office sits on the Obala Kulina Bana in the old town

Suggested itineraries

HALF-DAY: SARAJEVO IN A HURRY

It's always a good bet to start off at the Sebilj Fountain in Baščaršija and wander around the craftsmen's alleys. The coppersmith alley Kazandžiluk is a fascinating peek into Sarajevo's past and a great place to grab a handmade souvenir. From there it's wisest to head west up Sarači (which naturally turns into Ferhadija). Ferhadija carries on all the way up to the Eternal Flame on Maršala Tita with many of Sarajevo's most interesting attractions along the way.

1 DAY: TIME TO SEE A LITTLE MORE

With another half-day available be sure to check out the Sarajevo History Museum in Brusa Bezistan. Latinska Ćuprija (Latin Bridge) spans the River Miljacka not far from there; it was here that Franz Ferdinand was assassinated, sparking World War I. A 15–20 minute walk from there is the National Museum, which hosts the largest collection of exhibitions on Bosnia's cultural and natural history. If the time allows, the Tunnel Museum near Ilidža pays tribute to the only self-sustaining lifeline for the city during its four-year siege.

2–3 DAYS: TIME TO SEE MUCH MORE

Having the comfort of staying two to three days in Sarajevo you should not miss the opportunity to enjoy the café culture of the city. There are several spots for amazing panoramic views of Sarajevo – perhaps the best one being from the old Turkish fort or Bijela Tabija (White Garrison) on Vratnik. On the south side of the old town on Trebević Mountain are Kod Bibana and Park Prinčeva restaurants: they both have spectacular views of the

city and are great places for lunch, dinner or just a coffee. Make sure you take the tramway out to Ilidža as well, and stroll down or take a horse-and-carriage ride down Aleja towards the Vrelo Bosne Park.

LONGER: ENJOYING SARAJEVO TO THE FULL

If the opportunity presents itself the Olympic Mountains behind Sarajevo are absolutely stunning. Jahorina is geared more towards skiing and the winter season, whereas Bjelašnica has an amazing chain of highland villages, walking trails and mountain huts to complement its ski centre. Lukomir Village is one of Europe's last medieval villages. To the north of Sarajevo are the ancient medieval settlements of Kraljeva Sutjeska and Travnik.

Detail of the Peace Statue in Trg Oslobođenja

Something for nothing

One of the beauties of Sarajevo is that most of its cultural venues are comparatively cheap or free of charge. Most museums don't charge more than 2 KM for admission and galleries are usually free. The cinema is also cheap; Kino Obala often has local films that are usually subtitled in English.

The walking culture of Sarajevo makes long strolls around the city a fun event. People are always walking up and down with an occasional stop to shop or have coffee with friends. Aside from Ferhadija, there are areas to wander in every direction. To the north of town on Patriotske Lige, is the Olympic Stadium and Arena. Towards the west is Ilidža and the Vrelo Bosne Park, which has no entry fee. Aleja is the long oak-shaded walkway that leads to the park. The old residential parts of the city, Vratnik and Jekovac, are excellent places to catch a glimpse of old Sarajevo *mahalas* (quarters). Bijela Tabija (White Garrison) is an old fortification with perfect viewpoints for photography or just chilling out.

From Baščaršija you can also take the bus to Barice – for the price of just 2 KM this will take you from the valley at 526 m (1,725 ft) to over 1,000 m (3,280 ft) where there are delightful picnic and walking areas that offer some truly magnificent – not to say vertiginous – views. Just a 15-minute walk further up is Čavljak, where there are hiking trails, mountain lodges and a few cafés whose views are even more impressive, stretching 50 km (31 miles) and beyond. To the east of the old town, in the Miljacka Valley, is a long walking-path along the river.

Exploring Sarajevo's back streets costs nothing and can reveal hidden treasures

When it rains

When in Rome, do as the Romans do. Well, rainy days in Sarajevo never curb the café culture that dominates this city. Cafés are always rather busy regardless, but come a rainy day and the city flocks to them. The atmosphere is always chatty, light and fun, but be forewarned that Sarajevans are heavy smokers and most cafés and bars will be very smoky.

In the suburb of Ilidža there is a new indoor/outdoor swimming pool complex, the Terme Ilidža (see page 101), where you can enjoy swimming and/or sitting in a whirlpool or sauna. There is also a café and small restaurant there, making it an ideal place to spend the entire day. It is located on Butmirska Cesta. Tramways from the city centre to the last station in Ilidža run all day long. From the last tram stop it is a mere 5-minute walk.

The Zemaljski Muzej (see page 86), is by no means a grandiose museum but nonetheless has interesting exhibitions, particularly the ethnographic ones and the Haggadah, an ancient Jewish text brought from Spain in the late 15th century.

The Skenderija Shopping Centre (see page 89), is fairly large with mostly modern Western shops. There is also Brusa Bezistan in the old town. Although this is quite small, the shops are interesting enough for a couple of hours or so, including a coffee break. Just near the Brusa Bezistan shopping area is the Sarajevo History Museum. It too is tiny but is very well organised and interesting: exhibitions are also translated into English, unlike the National Museum, which has only a few exhibitions translated.

When the skies open, head into a café

On arrival

TIME DIFFERENCE

Bosnia and Herzegovina is on Central European Time (CET). It is one hour ahead of Greenwich Mean Time (GMT) in winter and British Summer Time (late Mar–end Oct).

ARRIVING

By air

Sarajevo Airport (ⓐ Kurta Schorka 36 ⓣ 033 289 121, 289 100 ⓦ www.sarajevo-airport.ba) is only 12 km (7½ miles) from the centre of town. There are no shuttle buses and no bus routes in the near vicinity; taxis will take you to town, usually for a fixed rate of 20 KM. You can change money in the airport at the bureau de change, and the post office sells phone cards if you need to contact your hotel or car hire company. If you intend to hire a car (see page 58), most car hire companies are located in the airport. The major hotels and even some of the smaller ones offer airport pick-up and drop-off. Fees vary.

By rail

The rail system was completely devastated during the war. It is now up and running but it is far from modern. There are regular connections from Ploče on the Croatian coast, Zagreb and Budapest. Internally, the rail system connects Mostar in the south and Zenica and Banja Luka to the north. The Bosnia and Herzegovina railway is now also a member of EuroRail, which means that travel passes are valid for Bosnia and Herzegovina as well. The train is generally slow but the views are spectacular.

Railway Station Sarajevo ⓐ Put Života 2 ⓣ 033 655 330

By road

The bus and train stations are located in the same place in the centre of town. Sarajevo is extremely well connected to the region and most of Europe by bus. Eurolines via Centrotrans runs regular buses to Sarajevo from all over western Europe. **Bus Station Sarajevo** (ⓐ Put Života 8 ⓣ 033 213 100, 213 010 ⓦ www.centrotrans.com) is centrally located very near the Holiday Inn. There are daily buses from Zagreb and Belgrade as well as most areas along the Croatian coast. There is both a taxi stand and a tramway stop that will take you downtown. A taxi ride won't cost more than 5 KM to the old town.

A tram passing through Marijin Dvar

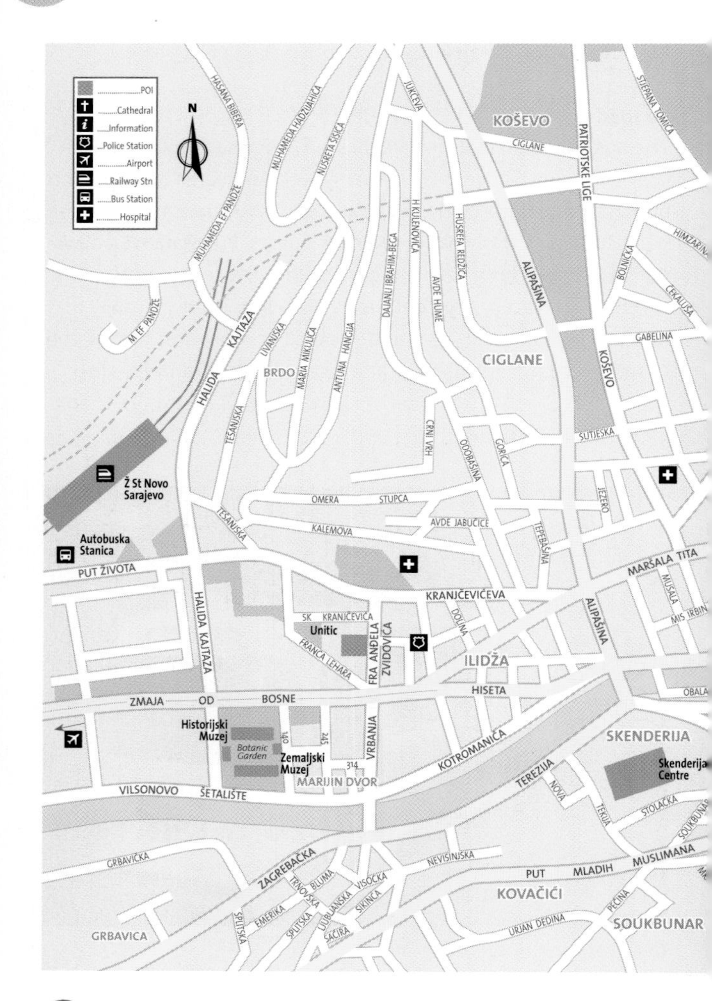
POI
Cathedral
Information
Police Station
Airport
Railway Stn
Bus Station
Hospital
N
KOŠEVO
CIGLANE
PATRIOTSKE LIGE
STJEPANA TOMIĆA
HASANA BIBERA
MUHAMEDA HADŽIJAHIĆA
NUSRETA ŠIŠIĆA
JUKIĆEVA
H KULENOVIĆA
HUSREFA REDŽIĆA
MUHAMEDA EF PANDŽE
M EF PANDŽE
DAJANLI IBRAHIM-BEGA
AVDE HUME
ALIPAŠINA
HIMZARINA
BOLNIČKA
ČEKALUŠA
GABELINA
KOŠEVO
CIGLANE
KAITAZA
HALIDA
LIVANJSKA
MARIA MIKULIĆA
ANTUNA HANGIJA
BRDO
TEŠANJSKA
CRNI VRH
ODOBAŠINA
GORICA
SUTJESKA
JEZERO
Ž St Novo Sarajevo
OMERA
STUPCA
TEŠANJSKA
KALEMOVA
AVDE JABUČICE
TEPEBAŠINA
Autobuska Stanica
PUT ŽIVOTA
MARŠALA TITA
MUSALA
MIS IRBINA
KRANJČEVIĆEVA
HALIDA KAJTAZA
SK KRANJČEVIĆA
Unitic
DOLINA
FRANCA LEHARA
FRA ANĐELA ZVIDOVIĆA
ALIPAŠINA
ILIDŽA
HISETA
OBALA
ZMAJA OD BOSNE
Historijski Muzej
Botanic Garden
Zemaljski Muzej
140
245
314
VRBANJA
SKENDERIJA
KOTROMANIĆA
Skenderija Centre
MARIJIN DVOR
VILSONOVO ŠETALIŠTE
TEREZIJA
NOVA
TEKIJA
STOLAČKA
SOUKBUNAR
GRBAVIČKA
ZAGREBAČKA
NEVISINJSKA
MUSLIMANA
PUT MLADIH
TRNOVSKA
BLUMA
VISOČKA
KOVAČIĆI
EMERIKA
SPLITSKA
SPLITSKA
LJUBLJANSKA
SIKINCA
ŠAČIRA
PEĆINA
URJAN DEDINA
SOUKBUNAR
GRBAVICA

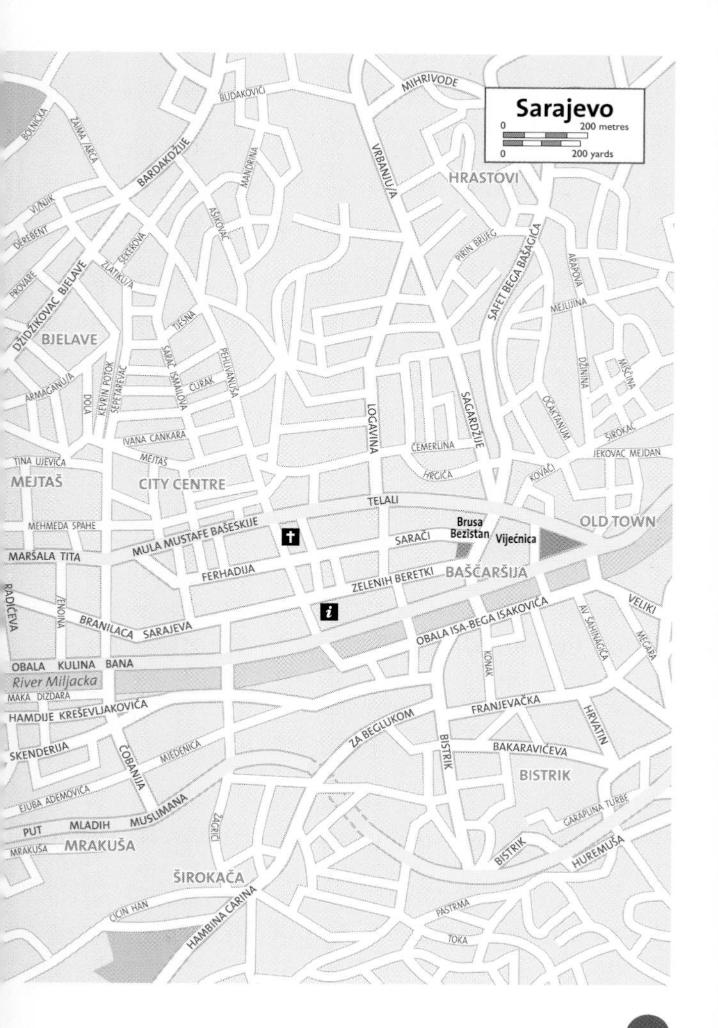
Sarajevo
0
200 metres
0
200 yards
MIHRIVODE
BUDAKOVIĆI
BOLNIČKA
ZAIMA ĆARĆA
BARDAKDŽIJE
MANDRINA
VRBANJUŠA
HRASTOVI
VIJENJIK
DEREBENT
ŠEKEROVA
ZLATIKUĆA
AŠIKOVAC
PIRIN BRIJEG
SAFET BEGA BAŠAGIĆA
ARAPOVA
MEJLIJINA
PROVARE
DŽIDŽIKOVAC
BJELAVE
TIJESNA
SARAČ ISMAILOVA
PEHLIVANUŠA
ĆURAK
DŽININA
MIŠČINA
ARMAGANUŠA
DOLA
KEVRIN POTOK
ŠEPETAREVAC
LOGAVINA
SAGARDŽIJE
OČAKTANUM
ŠIROKAC
IVANA CANKARA
MEJTAŠ
ČEMERLINA
JEKOVAC MEJDAN
TINA UJEVIĆA
HRGIĆA
KOVAČI
MEJTAŠ
CITY CENTRE
TELALI
MEHMEDA SPAHE
MULA MUSTAFE BAŠESKIJE
Brusa
Bezistan
Vijećnica
OLD TOWN
SARAČI
MARŠALA TITA
FERHADIJA
BAŠČARŠIJA
ZELENIH BERETKI
RADIĆEVA
ŽENOINA
VELIKI
BRANILACA SARAJEVA
OBALA ISA-BEGA ISAKOVIĆA
AV ŠAHINAGIĆA
MEĆARA
KONAK
OBALA KULINA BANA
River Miljacka
MAKA DIZDARA
HAMDIJE KREŠEVLJAKOVIĆA
FRANJEVAČKA
HRVATIN
ZA BEGLUKOM
SKENDERIJA
ČOBANIJA
MJEDENICA
BISTRIK
BAKARAVIĆEVA
BISTRIK
EJUBA ADEMOVIĆA
GARAPLINA TURBE
PUT MLADIH MUSLIMANA
ŽAGRIĆI
MRAKUŠA
MRAKUŠA
BISTRIK
HUREMUŠA
ŠIROKAČA
ĆIĆIN HAN
HAMBINA CARINA
PASTRMA
TOKA

Sarajevo is not very big and the main road (Zmaja od Bosne) running east–west in the valley should help you keep your bearings. Traffic can be a bit maddening in the mornings from 08.00 to 10.00 and in the afternoons between 15.00 and 17.00. Parking is often problematic in town. It is better to pay per hour for parking than to risk being towed away by the feared *pauk*. The *pauk*, meaning 'spider', is on regular patrol and will tow your car away without letting you know. It will cost over 100 KM to free your vehicle. Car theft does occur but not at the same rate as in most major cities. Practical precautions should be followed anywhere when travelling. If you have a nice, new car then secure it in a pre-paid car park where there are attendants.

FINDING YOUR FEET

Traffic in Sarajevo can be fairly hectic at times. The city has more cars than it has ever had, without the infrastructure to deal with it. Walking is the best bet, particularly as the main part of the city is in a flat valley. The residential areas tend to climb up the hills on the north and south sides of the valley. It is a surprisingly safe city with little crime. Be careful of pickpockets on the trams and trolleybuses as well as on the Ferhadija walkway or in crowded places.

ORIENTATION

Thanks to mother nature, navigating around Sarajevo is relatively straightforward. The old town and city centre are situated in the narrow valley of the River Miljacka. This valley consistently runs east–west. The river is the best landmark for keeping your bearings. It too runs east–west. The main road heading east is

IF YOU GET LOST, TRY ...

Do you speak English?
Da li govorite engleski?
Dah-lee goh-voh-ree-te ehn-glehskee?

Where is ...?
Gdje je ...?
Gdyeh-jee..?

On/to the left
Na lijevo
Na leeyevo

On/to the right
Na desno
Na desno

Obala Kulina Bana, which is one-way along the river all the way to the old town. It then circles back, remaining one-way, but with a few new name changes; in the old town it is Mula Mustafe Bašeskije, which turns into Maršala Tita at Vječna Vatra (Eternal Flame). People are extremely friendly and will readily help you if you get lost. Most young people speak English.

GETTING AROUND

The compact city centre makes it easy and enjoyable to do most moving around on foot. Pedestrians anywhere in Sarajevo need to be alert – zebra crossings or a green signal for pedestrians do not mean it is safe to cross the street.

The local bus system is the best in the country – run by GRAS it may, in fact, be the most efficiently operated state-owned enterprise – and, from Sarajevo, will get you to even the most isolated villages on Bjelašnica Mountain. Bus no. 31e runs the entire length of the city every half hour and costs around 2 KM

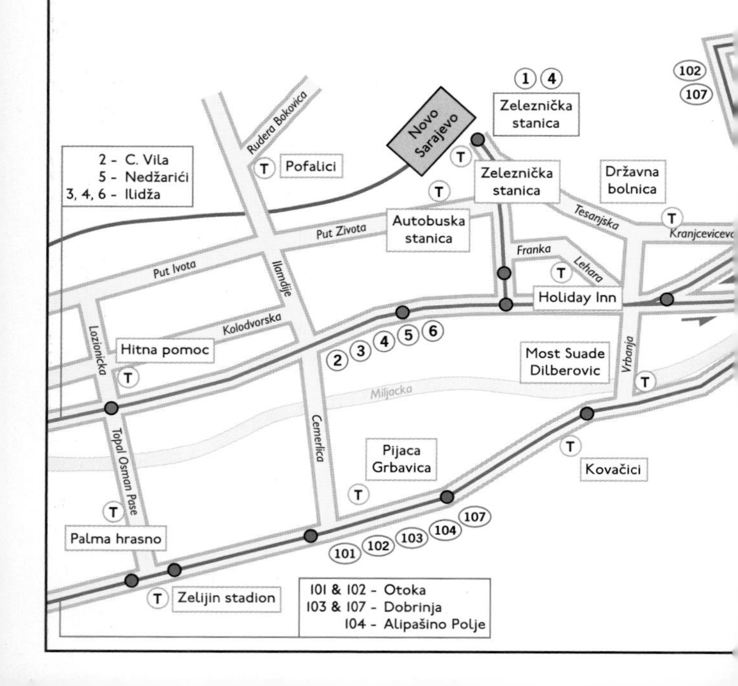
© Communicarta Ltd 2009 UDN.2
Map user Ref: WZFG/CS/SJJ/2006/66/4
Research and design by Robin Woods
2 - C. Vila
5 - Nedžarići
3, 4, 6 - Ilidža
Rudera Bokovica
Pofalici
Novo Sarajevo
Zeleznička stanica
Zeleznička stanica
Državna bolnica
Autobuska stanica
Put Zivota
Put Ivota
Tesanjska
Kranjcevićeva
Franka
Lehara
Ilamdije
Kolodvorska
Holiday Inn
Lozionicka
Hitna pomoc
Most Suade Dilberovic
Vrbanja
Miljacka
Cemerlica
Topal Osman Pase
Pijaca Grbavica
Kovačici
Palma hrasno
Zelijin stadion
101 & 102 - Otoka
103 & 107 - Dobrinja
104 - Alipašino Polje

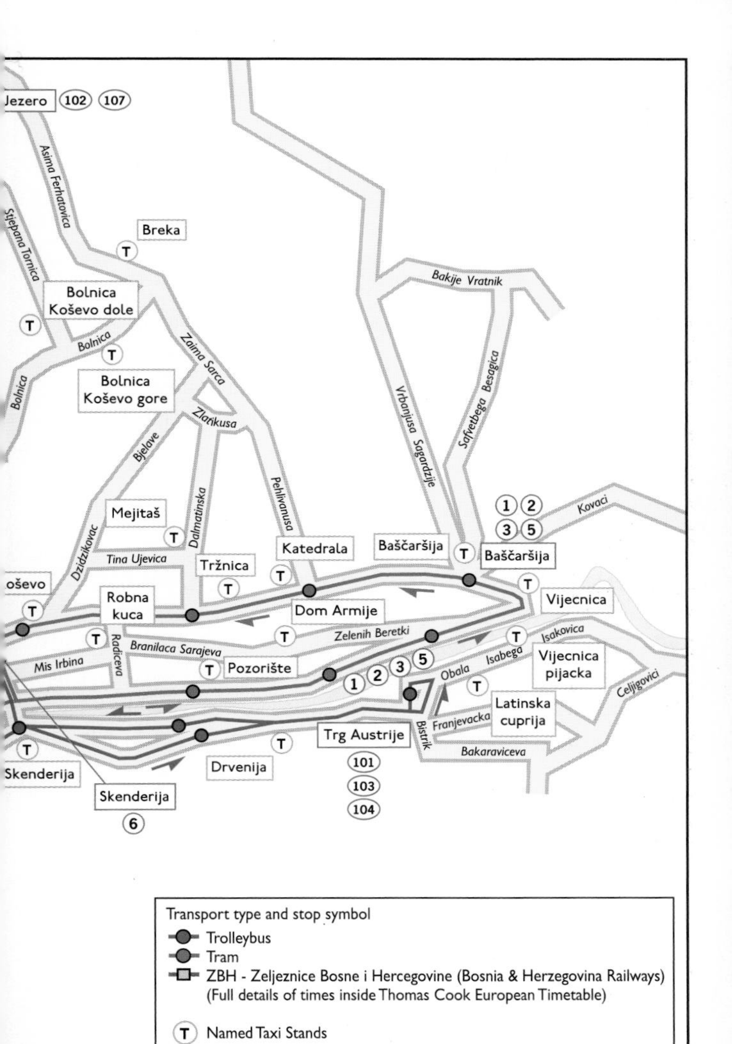

Jezero
102
107
Asima Ferhatovica
Stjepana Tornica
Breka
Bolnica Koševo dole
Bolnica
Bolnica
Bolnica Koševo gore
Zaima Sarca
Zlatikusa
Bjelave
Bakije Vratnik
Vrbanjusa Sagardzije
Safvetbega Besagica
Dalmatinska
Pehlivanusa
Mejitaš
Dzidzikovac
Tina Ujevica
Tržnica
Katedrala
Baščaršija
Baščaršija
Kovaci
1 2 3 5
ošević
Robna kuca
Dom Armije
Vijecnica
Zelenih Beretki
Isakovica
Isabega
Vijecnica pijacka
Radićeva
Branilaca Sarajeva
Mis Irbina
Pozorište
Obala
1 2 3 5
Celjigovici
Latinska cuprija
Franjevacka
Bistrik
Bakaraviceva
Trg Austrije
101
103
104
Drvenija
Skenderija
Skenderija
6
Transport type and stop symbol
Trolleybus
Tram
ZBH - Zeljeznice Bosne i Hercegovine (Bosnia & Herzegovina Railways)
(Full details of times inside Thomas Cook European Timetable)
T Named Taxi Stands

whether you are going one stop or all the way to the end. Starting by the National Archives and finishing in Dobrinja by the airport, it is the quickest, cleanest and easiest bus route in town. The 31e buses are yellow with a Japanese flag; they were donated to the city by the government of Japan.

The trams are also a reliable means of transportation, and constantly run up and down the main east–west road. There is also a tram station at the main bus/railway station, which operates all day. The tram lines extend all the way to Ilidža, a suburb to the west of Sarajevo, and for budget travellers it is a great way to check out the River Bosna Springs in Vrelo Bosne Park in Ilidža – it costs around 2 KM one way or you can buy a day pass for 4 KM. Tram nos. 1 and 4 go in the direction of the old town from the bus and railway stations.

Taxis are fairly inexpensive in Sarajevo.

Samir i Emir Taxi ⓐ Travnička 35 ⓣ 033 1516
Sarajevo Taxi ⓐ Azize Šaćirbegović 30A ⓣ 033 1515, 660 666

CAR HIRE

Bon Voyage ⓐ Trg Heroja 5 ⓣ/ⓕ 033 715 005 ⓦ www.bonvoyage.ba
Champion AC ⓐ Hamdije Kreševljakovića bb ⓣ 033 211 207 ⓦ www.cac-rent.ba
Europcar ⓐ Bulevar Meše Selimovića 16 ⓣ 033 450 961, 760 360 ⓦ www.europcar.ba
Unis ⓐ Ferhadija 16 ⓣ 033 222 239, 216 338 ⓦ www.unis-tours.ba

The Vijećnica (former City Hall) lit at night

THE CITY OF
Sarajevo

The Old Town

The old town of Sarajevo was largely built during the 400 years of Ottoman dominance in this region. Many of the quarters are markedly oriental, particularly the trading centre Baščaršija, which is the heart of the city's tourist area. It became a centre for trade as early as the late 15th century. The original old town, however, was up the northeastern hills just outside of Baščaršija at Kovači, Jekovac and Vratnik. The old city walls are located in this residential area with a wonderful maze of Ottoman-era tiny side streets through the various *mahalas* (neighbourhoods). The old town today has maintained much of its ancient flavour with the preservation of *stari zanati*, the old handicraftsmen, who have practised their trade on the same streets for centuries.

SIGHTS & ATTRACTIONS

With the exception of a few attractions high up on the surrounding hills, most things to see and do in the old town are walkable. Sarajevo is the perfect city for easy wanders and the old town is by far the most fascinating part.

Alifakovac

This is the neighbourhood across the River Miljacka near Vijećnica. It is famous for its hilltop cemetery that looks over the old town. It is here that Muslims from foreign lands were buried during Ottoman times. It is not uncommon to find people walking through this cemetery for a stroll and it's a great spot for photographing the old town. ⓐ Veliki Alifakovac

At-Mejdan Park

This beautiful square and park was once a gathering place for slave trading and public hangings; it was later transformed into a horse trading and racing area. Today it is a lovely park, with large trees and an Austro-Hungarian style pavilion for concerts, coffee and general gatherings. It is located on the south bank of the River Miljacka just across the Latin Bridge. ⓐ Obala Isa-bega Isakovića

Grave in the Muslim cemetery in Alifakovac

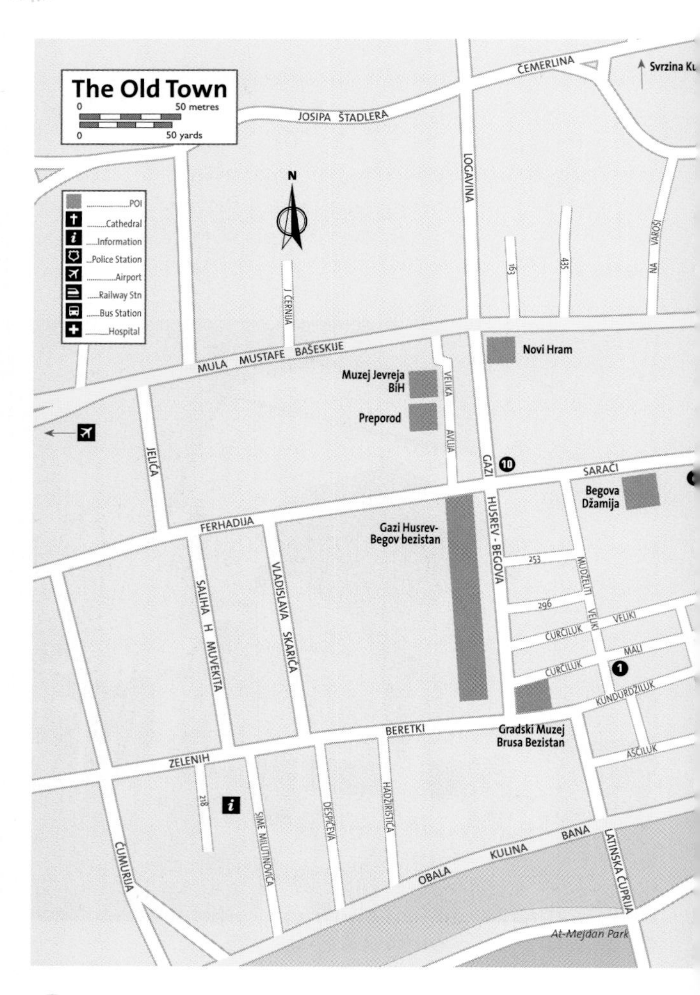
The Old Town
0
50 metres
0
50 yards
POI
Cathedral
Information
Police Station
Airport
Railway Stn
Bus Station
Hospital
N
ČEMERLINA
Svrzina Ku
JOSIPA ŠTADLERA
LOGAVINA
J ČERNIJA
163
435
NA VAROŠI
MULA MUSTAFE BAŠESKIJE
Novi Hram
Muzej Jevreja BiH
Preporod
VELIKA
AVLIJA
JELIĆA
GAZI
SARAČI
Begova Džamija
FERHADIJA
Gazi Husrev-Begov bezistan
HUSREV - BEGOVA
253
296
MUDŽELITI
VELIKI
ČURČILUK
MALI
ČURČILUK
KUNDURDŽILUK
SALIHA H MUVEKITA
VLADISLAVA SKARIĆA
BERETKI
Gradski Muzej Brusa Bezistan
AŠČILUK
ZELENIH
218
ŠIME MILUTINOVIĆA
DESPIĆEVA
HADŽIRISTIĆA
ĆUMURIJA
OBALA KULINA BANA
LATINSKA ĆUPRIJA
At-Mejdan Park

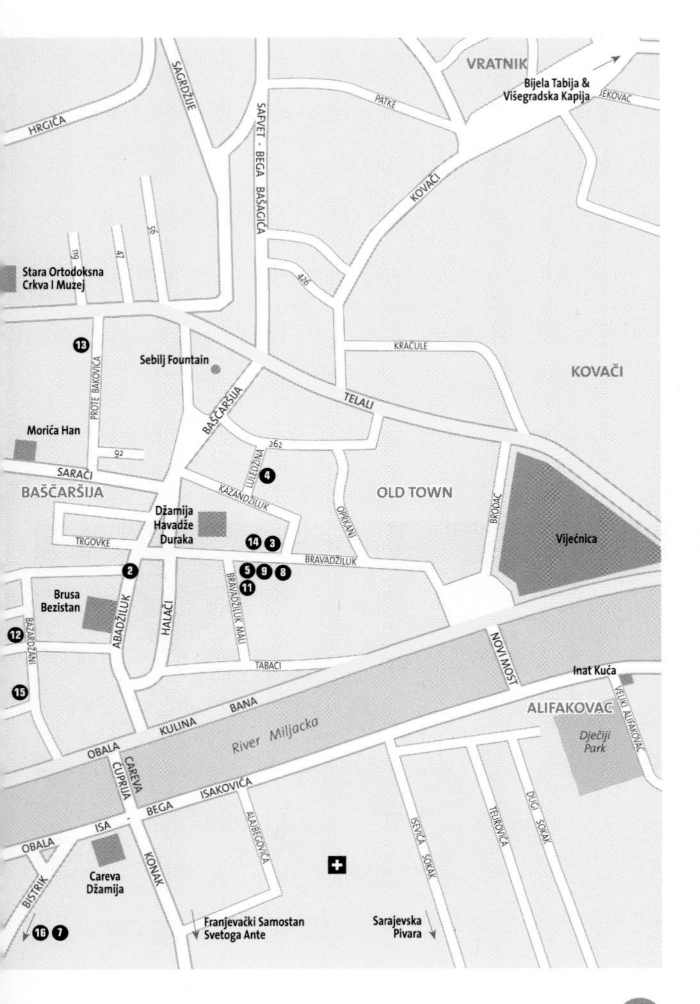

VRATNIK
Bijela Tabija & Višegradska Kapija
PATKE
HRGIĆA
SAGRDŽIJE
SAFVET - BEGA BAŠAGIĆA
KOVAČI
Stara Ortodoksna Crkva I Muzej
KRAČULE
KOVAČI
Sebilj Fountain
PROTE BAKOVIĆA
BAŠČARŠIJA
TELALI
Morića Han
262
SARAČI
BAŠČARŠIJA
LUEDŽINA
KAZANDŽILUK
OLD TOWN
Džamija Havadže Duraka
OPRKANJ
BRODAC
Vijećnica
TRGOVKE
BRAVADŽILUK
BRAVADŽILUK MALI
Brusa Bezistan
ABADŽILUK
HALAČI
BAZARDŽANI
NOVI MOST
TABACI
Inat Kuća
ALIFAKOVAC
VELIKI ALIFAKOVAC
BANA
KULINA
River Miljacka
Dječiji Park
OBALA
CAREVA ĆUPRIJA
ISAKOVIĆA
BEGA
ISA
OBALA
ALAJBEGOVIĆA
IŠEVIĆA SOKAK
TELJIROVIĆA
DUGI SOKAK
BISTRIK
Careva Džamija
KONAK
Franjevački Samostan Svetoga Ante
Sarajevska Pivara

Baščaršija

The hub of the trading centre in the old town. It has a distinct Turkish style to it and is the main attraction in Sarajevo. Here you will find the mosaic of trades that have been practised for centuries as well as beautiful fountains, mosques, churches and dozens of traditional eateries that both foreigners and locals flock to year round.

Begova Džamija (Gazi Husrev Bey's Mosque)

Situated on Sarači, this is considered to be the most significant Islamic structure in Bosnia and Herzegovina. It was built in 1531 with an endowment from Gazi Husrev Bey, the most famous Bosnian governor and the visionary largely responsible for Sarajevo becoming a city. The mosque is open to visitors, with

Spices for sale in Baščaršija

the exception of prayer time. Visitors are asked to enter from the side entrance and there are clear instructions on etiquette and photography posted in the mosque compound. ⓐ Sarači
🕒 10.00–17.00 Sat–Thur

Bijela Tabija (White Garrison)

This ancient fortification – reconstruction was completed in 2006 – has magnificent views of the entire city. Located in the high hills of the Vratnik neighbourhood, it is believed that this was some sort of fortification since the days of the Bosnian Kingdom. It was later reinforced and expanded by the Ottomans and its present-day look is of Austrian design. It was used to store ammunition and troops to defend the city during its many battles.
ⓐ Višegradska kapija

Brusa Bezistan

Built in 1551 by the Grand Vizier Rustempaša, the son-in-law of Sultan Sulejman the Magnificent, this building was named for being a centre for silk trade from Brusa in Asia Minor. It is now completely restored after being damaged in the conflict and is a shopping area for antiques and handicrafts. ⓐ Abadžiluk 10
🕒 08.00–20.00 Mon–Fri, 09.00–14.00 Sat

Careva Džamija (Czar's Mosque)

Originally a wooden structure built in 1457 in honour of Sultan Mehmed II, the current structure was built in 1566 and restored many times since. Today it is the main mosque for Sarajevo's Islamic leadership. Like most of the old Ottoman-style mosques in the old town, it is endowed with a beautiful courtyard and

garden. It is open on some occasions but not regularly for guests. ⓐ Obala Isa-bega Isakovića

Džamija Havadže Duraka (Baščaršija Mosque)

Located in the main square near Sebilj Fountain. It is believed to have been built before 1528 and is renowned for two things – its beautiful rose garden and being one of the few mosques in the country where the call to prayer is still done live and not recorded or over a microphone. ⓐ Baščaršija ⓞ 09.00–20.00 Sat–Thur

Franjevački Samostan Svetoga Ante (Franciscan Monastery & Church of St Ante)

The monastery was built in neo-Gothic style by Karlo Panek in the early years of Austrian rule while the church was designed by the famous architect Josip Vancas in 1914. It is located in the Bistrik neighbourhood just next to the brewery on Franjevačka street. The monastery hosts a large number of old manuscripts, books, paintings and handicrafts. The church is open to visitors and there is a souvenir and book shop at the entrance.
ⓐ Franjevačka 6 ⓣ 033 236 107 ⓦ www.svantosarajevo.org
ⓞ 08.00–18.00

Inat Kuća (Spite House)

There is an interesting story behind its present location. When the Austrians sanitised the River Miljacka at the turn of the 20th century they intended to knock down several houses. One homeowner refused and would only accept if the house, once located on the northern bank, was relocated – stone by stone – to the south bank. It is now a popular restaurant with a sign at

Baščaršija Mosque at night

the entrance reading 'I was once located on the other side, but out of spite I moved over here'. ⓐ Veliki Alifakovac ⓣ 033 447 867 ⓛ 11.00–22.30

Kazandžiluk

This street has managed to maintain and preserve much of its intended function and appearance. Five centuries of coppersmiths have practised their skills here, with this unique trade passed on from father to son since the 16th century. They specialise in the traditional Bosnian coffee and tea sets as well as carved plates of Sarajevo skyline motifs.

Latinska Ćuprija (Latin Bridge)

The bridge has stood since 1565. It linked the Catholic *mahala* to the central trading area. It did not become famous, however, until 1914 when Gavrilo Princip assassinated Archduke Franz Ferdinand and his pregnant wife. This deed sparked World War I. Despite its fame for the assassination it is one of the finest examples of the superiority of Ottoman bridge architecture. ⓐ Obala Kulina Bana

Morića Han

A must-see place while visiting the old town. The old inn received guest traders from Dubrovnik and the east throughout the Ottoman era. It was built as a free inn, where traders with their horses and caravans could stay without charge. Today it houses a Persian rug centre as well as a restaurant and café. ⓐ Sarači 77 ⓣ 033 236 119 ⓛ 07.00–22.00

Sarači

This was the first street founded in Sarajevo, and is the main pedestrian walkway in the city. Its name is derived from the leatherworkers that traded here since the mid-16th century. Its natural extension is Ferhadija.

Sarajevska Pivara (Sarajevo Brewery)

Most Sarajevans will confirm that this brewery is more than just a brewery. Built during Austro-Hungarian rule in 1881 by the wealthy Viennese industrialist Heinrich Levi, it has since become a landmark not only of good beer but for helping to save the city of Sarajevo. The brewery was built on a water source that enabled many citizens of Sarajevo to access clean water during the marathon siege from 1992–5. A new restaurant and bar serves good food and the country's only dark beer. ⓐ Franjevačka 15, Bistrik ⓣ 033 491 100 ⓦ www.sarajevska-pivara.ba ⓒ 10.00–16.00 Sun–Fri

Sebilj Fountain

The landmark of the old town. It has been a meeting place since the 16th century when traders would come from both East and West. It is also better known as pigeon square due to the great number of pigeons that nest in the large poplar trees overhanging the fountain. Sebilj has been renovated after having been slightly damaged during the conflict. It's a great area to sit and drink Bosnian coffee or *smreka*, a juice made from juniper berries. ⓐ Baščaršija

Svrzina Kuća (Svrzo's House)

This is a beautifully preserved 18th-century Ottoman house, but although built in Ottoman style, it has a distinctly Bosnian feel to it. You can explore the house on your own, but it is recommended that you take the guided tour to hear the fascinating stories about the shower system, the furniture, the dining arrangements, the kitchen, the all-important privacy and, more generally, the dynamics of a wealthy family in Ottoman times. ⓐ Glodžina 8 ⓣ 033 535 264 ⓦ www.muzejsarajeva.ba ⓛ 10.00–17.00 Tues–Sat, 10.00–13.00 Sun. Admission charge

Vijećnica (former City Hall/National Library)

Up to the onset of the war, this was the National Library and Archives of Bosnia and Herzegovina. Before that it was the city hall during Austro-Hungarian rule. Vijećnica is located on Obala Kulina Bana along the river at the back end of Bravadžiluk where all the *ćevapi* and *burek* shops are. It was from here that Franz Ferdinand's caravan began their fateful parade before he was shot in 1914 on Latin Bridge (see page 68). This pseudo-Moorish 19th-century construction was bombed with phosphor in 1992 and is one of the few major landmarks of Sarajevo not to be fully restored. There are frequent art exhibitions in the main hall and admission is free. ⓐ Obala Kulina Bana ⓛ 10.00–17.00 Tues–Sat, 10.00–13.00 Sun

Višegradska Kapija (Višegrad Gate)

The Vratnik neighbourhood of Sarajevo was the original residential area of the city. The old walls of the city can still be seen in places as well as many arched gateways. The Višegrad Gate was a heavily guarded entrance and exit to the city during

Ottoman times. It opened towards the old passage to the eastern town of Višegrad on the border with Serbia. It is located just next to the Bijela Tabija (White Garrison). ⓐ Višegradska kapija

CULTURE

Gradski Muzej Brusa Bezistan (City Museum Brusa Bezistan)
This relatively new museum was completed in 2004. It is situated right in the centre of town, in a beautiful six-dome Ottoman building. The collection – costumes, coins, tombstones and other items you would expect to find in a historical museum – is tastefully exhibited and accompanied with interesting texts in excellent English. ⓐ Kundurdžiluk 10 ⓣ 033 475 740, 475 741 ⓦ www.muzejsarajeva.ba ⓛ 10.00–17.00 Tues–Sat, 10.00–13.00 Sun. Admission charge

Musej Jevreja BiH (Jewish Museum)
When the Jews were expelled from Spain in the late 15th century it was the Ottoman Empire that welcomed them and placed them throughout the empire. The arrival, lifestyle and treatment of the Jews that settled in and around Sarajevo are told through this museum. The texts are in good English and the material is exhibited well, using each of the three floors of this renovated cobblestone building in the centre of town. ⓐ Velika Avlija ⓣ 033 33 535 688 ⓦ www.muzejsarajeva.ba ⓛ 10.00–17.00. Admission charge

Novi Hram
This building was originally a synagogue. It was given to the

community as a present so that it could become a gallery space. ⓐ Mula Mustafe Bafieskije 38 ⓣ 033 233 280 ◷ 15.00–19.00 Sun–Fri

Preporod

This commercial gallery houses work by local and regional artists working in various media from etching to oils. There are many images depicting Bosnian and Sarajevan scenes and landscapes. ⓐ Velika Avlija ⓣ 033 445 196 ◷ 09.00–21.00 Mon–Sat

Stara Ortodoksna Crkva I Muzej (Old Orthodox Church & Museum)

This church is believed to have been built on the ancient foundations of an early Christian *hram* (place of worship). Located in the heart of the old town, this house of worship is best known for its very large iconostasis covering the entire right-hand wall. The accompanying museum is well lit and has a more modern feel to it. It features Bibles, paintings, frescoes, ceremonial ornaments and a few gowns, all from the period between the 15th and 18th centuries. The church itself does not charge an entry fee. ⓐ Mula Mustafe Bašeskije 59 ⓣ 033 571 761 ◷ Museum: 10.00–15.00 Tues–Sun (except Orthodox holidays); church: 08.00–17.00. Admission charge to museum only

RETAIL THERAPY

Given that the Baščaršija part of the old town is an ancient trading centre, what else can you do but shop? And Baščaršija is *the* place to find authentic handicrafts. Be sure to wander through the labyrinth of narrow side streets, there may be surprises around any corner. This area is void of shopping centres or malls but has literally hundreds of small shops selling a wide variety of handmade crafts. Sarači street in the old town is lined with little shops selling gold, silver, leather, carpets and other high-quality products. Brusa Bezistan, the old silk trading centre located just where the stone walkway turns 'modern', houses dozens of tiny shops under its six-dome roof.

There are also many shops in the old town designed to 'give back' to the community and support women's groups. The **Bosnian Handicraft Knitwear Shop** (Čizmedžiluk 1 08.00–20.00 Mon–Fri, 09.00–19.00 Sat, 10.00–16.00 Sun) sells handmade sweaters, gloves, scarves and toys made by Bosnian women. **Melanie Gift Shop** (Sime Milutinovića 15 033 667 836 10.00–19.00 Mon–Fri, 10.00–15.00 Sat) has beautiful pictures, souvenirs and handmade cards. There are also dozens of small art galleries exhibiting the works of local artists. You can find some great deals on paintings of authentically local motifs. Vendors don't mind bargaining as well, so don't be shy.

Along Ferhadija after Gazi Husrev-Begova, shopping turns markedly Western. Many of the most famous and popular retail shops are located along this Viennese-style walkway. Brand name clothes are not particularly cheap in Sarajevo but Italian and leather shoes are said to be significantly less expensive than in the West.

TAKING A BREAK

Sarajevo's old town is dominated by *buregdžinicas, ćevabžinicas* and traditional restaurants. The aroma of the Baščaršija area is enough to make your mouth water. There are literally dozens of places for inexpensive lunch and/or coffee breaks. Here are just a few of the best spots: all of them are walkable.

Aščinica ASDŽ £ ❶ This is a cafeteria-type place with a fresh selection of traditional Bosnian dishes. You can pick what you like at the counter and the waiter will bring your meal to the table. ⓐ Ćurčiluk Mali 3 ⓣ 033 238 500 ⓛ 08.00–19.00

Badem £ ❷ An oriental spice, sweet and nut shop. If you're just up for a quick snack you can find sweet almonds, pistachios, peanuts, Turkish delights and a large variety of oriental treats. ⓐ Abadžiluk 12 ⓣ 033 533 135 ⓛ 08.00–23.00

Bosna £ ❸ One of the classic pita places in the old town. It's always crowded – and for a reason: the pita is baked fresh all day and the service is quick and friendly. ⓐ Bravadžiluk 11 ⓣ 033 538 426 ⓛ 08.00–22.00

Halvat £ ❹ No food here but the best-kept secret in the heart of the old town: this teashop is similar to the *shisha* places found in Istanbul. It serves Turkish, Moroccan and other teas as well as Bosnian coffee. The *shishas*, or water pipes, are packed with apple- or honey-flavoured tobacco. ⓐ Luledžina 6 ⓣ 061 515 713 ⓛ 09.00–23.00

Hodžić £ ❺ There is a stretch of restaurants on Bravadžiluk serving *ćevapi* (sausages) and other Bosnian meat dishes. They're all good. Hodžić serves fine quality meats at very low prices.

ⓐ Bravadžiluk 34 ⓣ 033 532 866 ⓒ 08.00–22.30

Kebab £ ❻ For doner kebab Turkish style this is a great place to go. The meat is fresh and tasty, and this is a perfect place for a quick break where one can people-watch as well. ⓐ Čizmedžiluk 21 ⓒ 09.00–22.00

Kod Bibana £ ❼ It's best to pay a bit for the taxi ride because it's quite far up the hill on the southern slopes of the old town. The views are magnificent and the food is wholesome and tasty. It's a laidback place and a favourite spot for locals young and old. ⓐ Hošin brijeg 95 ⓣ 033 232 026 ⓒ 10.00–22.00 ⓘ No credit cards

Mrkva £ ❽ The name means carrot, but this is another one of the classic *ćevapi* (sausages) and meat speciality spots. The name doesn't represent what it sells; if you like meat, you'll like Mrkva. ⓐ Bravadžiluk 13 ⓣ 033 532 519 ⓒ 08.00–22.00

Petica £ ❾ The name means 5, the highest grade a student can get in school. This place claims to have to the best *ćevapi* (sausages) in town. It is certainly among the best of Sarajevo's long list of *ćevabdžinicas*. ⓐ Bravadžiluk 29 ⓣ 033 537 555 ⓒ 07.00–22.00

Ramis £ ❿ The legendary sweet shop of Sarajevo. It is located just on the artificial border where the old Turkish quarters ends and the Austro-Hungarian part begins. Cakes, made fresh daily, and coffee are very inexpensive. ⓐ Sarači 1 ⓣ 033 535 947 ⓒ 09.00–22.00

Sač £ ⓫ This is one of the few places in the old town where they make pita the old way, in the 'Dutch oven', baked with coals in a large metal pan. Every sort of pita is delicious and you can see the way it is made at the front counter. ⓐ Bravadžiluk Mali 2 ⓣ 061 439 045 ⓒ 08.00–23.00

Željo £ ⓬ It is said that you haven't visited Sarajevo if you haven't eaten *ćevapi* (sausages) at Željo. Željo is named after the local football club. ⓐ Kundurdžiluk 12 ⓣ 033 447 000 ⓒ 08.00–22.00

AFTER DARK

RESTAURANTS

Pod Lipom £ ⓭ Some of the best traditional food in the old town. Pod Lipom has been around for ages and is a favourite spot for locals. For price it's definitely one of the best deals in town. ⓐ Prote Bakovića 8 i 6 ⓣ 033 440 700 ⓒ 08.00–00.00 ⓘ No credit cards

Bosanska Kuća ££ ⓮ Although this place is a bit 'touristy' the food and service are truly excellent. It's one of the few places in the heart of Baščaršija that you can have a beer with lunch. The steaks and veal dishes are their speciality. ⓐ Bravadžiluk 3 ⓣ 033 237 320 ⓦ www.bosnianhouse.com ⓒ 09.00–01.00

Hacienda Cantina Mexicana ££ ⓯ Hacienda is the only Mexican restaurant in the centre of the city. Downstairs is one of the best bars in town. ⓐ Bazardžani 3 ⓣ 033 441 918 ⓦ www.placetobe.ba ⓒ 10.00–23.00 Mon–Fri, 10.00–01.00 Sat & Sun ⓘ No credit cards

Park Prinčeva ££ ⓰ Try to arrive before sunset when dining here: this restaurant boasts the best view in town and certainly has the food and atmosphere to match. There is often soft, live traditional music, which goes perfectly with the traditional menu. ⓐ Iza Hrida 7 ⓣ 061 222 708 ⓦ www.parkprinceva.ba ⓛ 09.00–23.30

To Be ££ ⓱ This tiny restaurant is on one of the many sidestreets in the old town. The food is top grade, as is the service. To Be has a very cosy and intimate atmosphere and is perfect for couples. The vegetarian soup is fantastic, as are the steak and vegetarian platters. ⓐ Čizmedžiluk 5 ⓣ 033 233 265 ⓛ 12.00–23.00 ⓘ No credit cards

BARS & CLUBS

Baghdad Café One of the old town's newest bars. It's a bit on the pricey side for Sarajevo but serves good cocktails in a comfy and unique Arabesque setting. ⓐ Bazardžani 6 ⓣ 061 170 880 ⓦ www.baghdadcafe.ba ⓛ 10.00–02.00

City Pub A spacious and happening place that could quite possibly be the best bar in town. Great drink prices, a friendly atmosphere and frequent live music/DJs. Entrance on Zelenih beretki. ⓐ Hadžiristića bb ⓣ 033 209 789 ⓦ www.citypub.co.ba ⓛ 10.00–02.00

The City Centre

For the purpose of this book the border between the old town and the centre is the square around the Cathedral. Although most parts of the old town and centre are intimately linked, the division is marked around municipal borders and based, to a large extent, on the era of their establishment. The city centre is the political and administrative hub of Sarajevo. It was largely built at the beginning of the 20th century when Bosnia and Herzegovina was part of the Austro-Hungarian empire, and has a distinct Viennese feel to it – the architecture and urban layout differs very much from that of the old Turkish-era quarters. This area was heavily damaged during the war but has since received a very attractive facelift with new façades of many colours, pavements and asphalted roads.

SIGHTS & ATTRACTIONS

As a natural extension from the old town the sights and attractions in the city centre are all rather compact and easy to access by foot. Ferhadija eventually merges with Maršala Tita near the Eternal Flame; this is a good reference point for wandering and easily finding your way back towards the old town. Parallel to Maršala Tita to the south is the River Miljacka. It runs in a clear east–west direction in the valley, acting as a good orientation landmark.

Bošnjački Institut

Originally a *hamam* from the 16th century, the new Bosniac Institute is now a foundation dedicated to the preservation and promotion of Bosnian Muslim cultural heritage in Bosnia and Herzegovina. There are several art exhibitions, frequent concerts, and one of the largest libraries in the city. It is located just behind the Cathedral. ⓐ Mula Mustafe Bafieskije 21 ⓣ 033 279 800 ⓦ www.bosnjackiinstitut.org ⓛ 10.00–14.00 Sat for pre-booked tours

Crkva Sv Ćirila I Metoda (Church of St Cyril & Methodius)
Located just behind the Cathedral on Josipa Stadlera street this church and seminary is quite an interesting building. The church is the centrepiece of the structure, with two wings very skilfully added on by the architect Josip Vancaš in 1895. It is the main seminary in Bosnia for students of Catholic theology. ⓐ Josipa Stadlera ⓛ 07.30–20.00

Ferhadija
Sarajevo wouldn't be Sarajevo without Ferhadija. The pastime of long walks and strolls with friends and family is sacred in this city. Ferhadija marks the first European influences on the city with the arrival of the Austro-Hungarian Empire in 1878. Much resembling Vienna with its beautiful architecture, the walkway is lined with Western shops and cafés and is bustling at all hours of the day.

Katedrala (Cathedral)
The Sacred Heart of Jesus Cathedral was built in 1889. Its architectural design was inspired by the Notre Dame of Dijon in France. As a centrepiece of Sarajevo's multi-confessional culture the Katedrala is a famous meeting place. Many young people hang out on the steps or wait for friends here. The church is open for

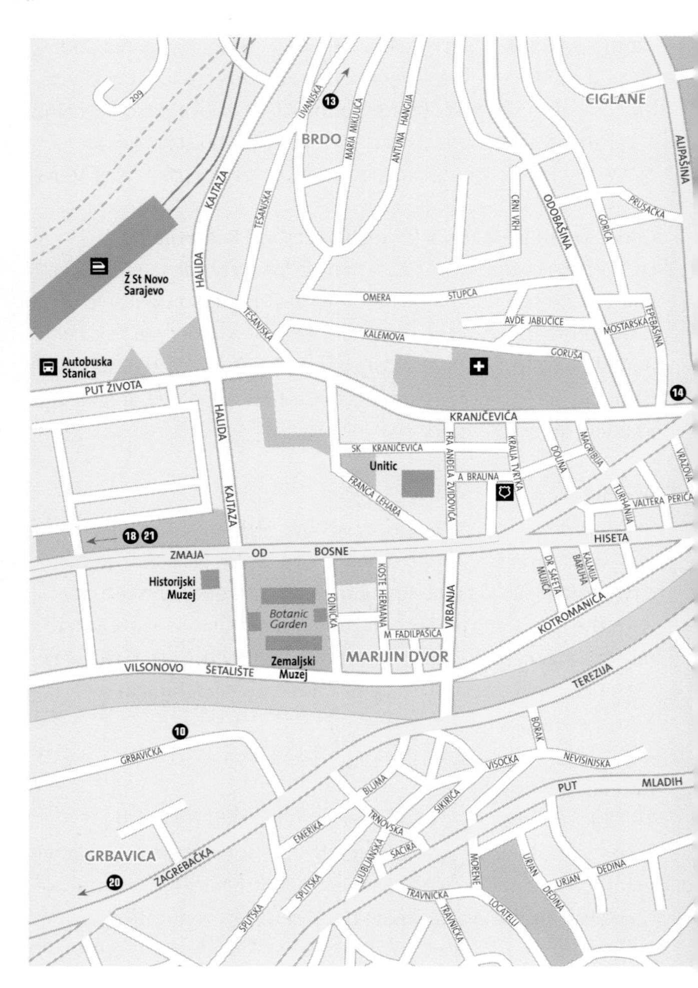

209
UVANJSKA
13
BRDO
MARIA MIKULIĆA
ANTUNA HANGIJA
CIGLANE
ALIPAŠINA
KAJTAZA
TEŠANJSKA
CRNI VRH
ODOBAŠINA
PRUSAČKA
GORICA
Ž St Novo Sarajevo
HALIDA
OMERA
STUPCA
AVDE JABUČICE
TEPEBAŠINA
MOSTARSKA
TEŠANJSKA
KALEMOVA
GORUŠA
Autobuska Stanica
PUT ŽIVOTA
14
KRANJČEVIĆA
HALIDA
SK KRANJČEVIĆA
FRA ANĐELA ŽVIZDOVIĆA
KRALJA TVRTKA
DOLINA
MAGRIBIJA
VRAZOVA
Unitic
A BRAUNA
FRANCA LEHARA
KAJTAZA
TURHANIJA
VALTERA PERIĆA
18
21
HISETA
ZMAJA
OD
BOSNE
DR SAFETA MUJIĆA
KALMIJA BARUHA
Historijski Muzej
KOSTE HERMANA
FOJNIČKA
Botanic Garden
VRBANJA
KOTROMANIĆA
M FADILPAŠIĆA
MARIJIN DVOR
VILSONOVO
ŠETALIŠTE
Zemaljski Muzej
TEREZIJA
10
BORAK
GRBAVIČKA
VISOČKA
NEVISINJSKA
BLUMA
PUT
MLADIH
SIKIRIĆA
TRNOVSKA
EMERIKA
ŠAĆIRA
GRBAVICA
ZAGREBAČKA
LJUBLJANSKA
MORENE
URIJAN
DEDINA
URIJAN
DEDINA
20
SPLITSKA
TRAVNIČKA
TRAVNIČKA
LOCATELI
SPLITSKA

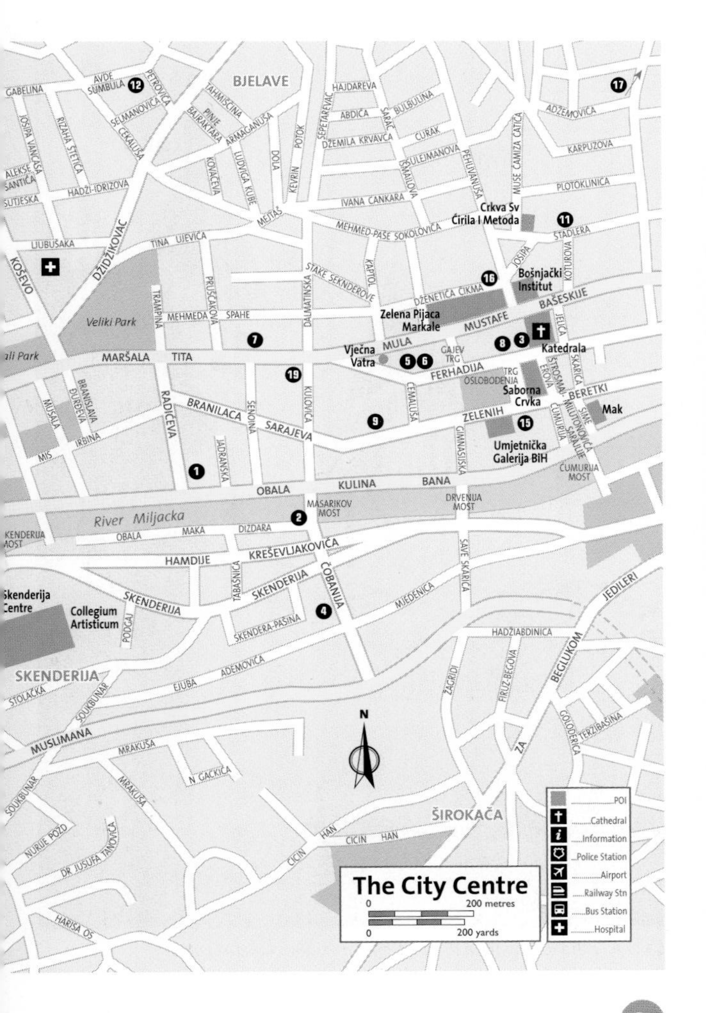
BJELAVE
GABELINA
AVDE SUMBULA
PETROVIĆA
SELMANOVIĆA
ČEKALUŠA
JOSIPA VANČAŠA
RIZAHA ŠTETIĆA
ALEKSE ŠANTIĆA
SUTJESKA
HADŽI-IDRIZOVA
LJUBUŠAKA
KOŠEVO
DŽIDŽIKOVAC
HAJDAREVA
ABDIĆA
BULBULINA
DŽEMILA KRVAVCA
ČURAK
SULEJMANOVA
ŠEPETAREVAC
ŠARAČ
DOLA
POTOK
KEVRIN
LUDVIGA KUBE
KOVAČEVA
ARMAGANUŠA
PINJE BAJRAKTARA
MEJTAŠ
IVANA CANKARA
ŠMAILOVA
PEHLIVANUŠA
MUSE ĆAMIZA ĆATIĆA
ADŽEMOVIĆA
KARPUZOVA
PLOTOKLINIĆA
Crkva Sv Ćirila I Metoda
STADLERA
MEHMED-PAŠE SOKOLOVIĆA
TINA UJEVIĆA
KAPTOL
STAKE ŠEKNDEROVE
JOSIPA
KOTUROVA
Bošnjački Institut
DŽENETIĆA ČIKMA
BAŠESKIJE
TRAMPINA
PRUŠČAKOVA
DALMATINSKA
MEHMEDA
SPAHE
Veliki Park
Zelena Pijaca Markale
MUSTAFE
JELIĆA
Katedrala
MARŠALA TITA
ali Park
Vječna Vatra
MULA
GAJEV TRG
FERHADIJA
TRG OSLOBOĐENJA
Saborna Crvka
ŠTROSMAJEROVA
SKARIĆA
BERETKI
Mak
BRANISLAVA ĐURĐEVA
MUSALA
RADIČEVA
BRANILACA
ŠENOINA
KULOVIĆA
SARAJEVA
ČEMALUŠA
ZELENIH
GIMNAZIJSKA
ČUMURIJA
SIME MILUTINOVIĆA SARAJLIJE
IRBINA
MIS
JADRANSKA
Umjetnička Galerija BiH
ČUMURIJA MOST
OBALA KULINA BANA
MASARIKOV MOST
DRVENIJA MOST
River Miljacka
KENDERIJA MOST
OBALA
MAKA
DIZDARA
HAMDIJE
KREŠEVLJAKOVIĆA
SAVE SKARIĆA
TABAŠNICA
SKENDERIJA
ČOBANIJA
Skenderija Centre
Collegium Artisticum
PODGAJ
SKENDERA-PAŠINA
MJEDENICA
JEDILERI
HADŽIABDINICA
BEGLUKOM
SKENDERIJA
ADEMOVIĆA
EJUBA
STOLAČKA
SOUKBUNAR
ZAGRIDI
FIRUZ-BEGOVA
GOLODERICA
TERZIBAŠINA
MUSLIMANA
MRAKUŠA
N. GACKIĆA
N
ZA
SOUKBUNAR
ŠIROKAČA
NURIJE POZD
DR JUSUFA TANOVIĆA
HAN
ČIČIN HAN
ČIČIN
HARISA OS
The City Centre
0 200 metres
0 200 yards
POI
Cathedral
Information
Police Station
Airport
Railway Stn
Bus Station
Hospital

The Catholic Katedrala (Cathedral) is a famous meeting place

visitors when there is no mass. ⓐ Fra Grge Martića bb, off Ferhadija ⓣ 033 210 281 ⓛ 08.30–16.00 Sun & Mon

Saborna Crkva

The city's largest Orthodox Church. It was built during the last few years of Ottoman rule in 1868. The church is an interesting combination of neo-baroque and Byzantium styles. The interior is rather dark and full of mystique, quite different from the style of Catholic churches. ⓐ Trg Oslobođenja ⓛ 08.00–20.00 Mon–Sat

Trg Oslobođenja (Liberation Square)

This is also a popular hangout for both young and old. Located just off Ferhadija, this square is home to the Orthodox Church, the National Gallery and the Economics Faculty. It is perhaps most well known for its elderly chess players who religiously play on the large chessboard painted in the square. Trg Oslobođenja also hosts a honey and medicinal herb festival during the summer.

Veliki Park

One of only a few of Sarajevo's parks to have survived the war. Many of the city's large trees were chopped down during the conflict to be used for cooking and heating. This green area has been a park since the 16th century, and is very near the Presidency on Maršala Tita. It's an ideal place to chill out or grab a snack and make a picnic. ⓐ Maršala Tita

Vječna Vatra (Eternal Flame)

Situated at the very beginning of Ferhadija, this national monument pays homage to the liberators of Sarajevo during

The Vječna Vatra (Eternal Flame) commemorates the World War II dead

World War II. The commemoration was constructed just after the city was liberated on 6 April 1945. ⓐ Ferhadija

Zelena Pijaca Markale (Markale Produce Market)

Markale was beamed across our television screens in 1995 when a mortar round slammed into this busy marketplace killing 68 people. There is a memorial plaque on the back wall of the marketplace with all the names of the victims from this atrocity. The market itself sells fresh produce from the early morning. ⓐ Mula Mustafe Bafieskije ⓑ 07.00–17.00

CULTURE

Collegium Artisticum

Located in the Skenderija Shopping Centre, this gallery often hosts art exhibitions and contemporary art shows. There is a café next door where many of Sarajevo's 'old school' artistic crowd still gather. Terezija bb 033 270 752 www.collegium.ba 10.00–18.00 Mon–Sat

Historijski Muzej (Sarajevo History Museum)

The contrast with its beautiful Austro-Hungarian neighbour in which the National Museum is housed could not be more pronounced. The Historical Museum is located in a much smaller socialist era building to the west of the Zemaljski Muzej. On the ground floor, this museum has two small exhibitions: the one on the recent war is impressive simply due to the fact that it is a 'fresh' topic but otherwise lacks style, variety and content. The upper part of the museum hosts a modern art exhibition. Zmaja od Bosne 5 033 210 418 http://historijski.muzej.ba 09.00–14.00 Tues–Fri, 09.00–13.00 Sat & Sun. Admission charge

Mak

This gallery serves a double purpose – it is also the literature museum of Bosnia and Herzegovina. It frequently has exhibitions displaying paintings of all genres, hosts book launches and promotions, as well as theatre exhibitions and performance art. Sime Milutinovića Sarajlije 7 033 471 828 10.00–19.00 Mon–Fri, 10.00–15.00 Sat & Sun

Umjetnička Galerija BiH (National Gallery of Bosnia & Herzegovina)
The National Gallery has a permanent exhibition of both old and contemporary paintings and sculptures, all made by Bosnian artists. In addition, there are temporary exhibitions, differing widely in nature and quality. It is by far the best place to view the most of Bosnia and Herzegovina's most influential artists of the 20th century. In the ground-floor gallery there are frequent modern exhibitions and the occasional soft jazz concert. ⓐ Zelenih Beretki 8 ⓣ 033 266 550, 266 651
◷ 12.00–20.00 Tues–Sat

Zemaljski Muzej (National Museum)
This museum, like most other things in Sarajevo, came out of the war looking battered. But its exterior has been renovated. These four Austro-Hungarian buildings do not look their age (120 years) and would make this museum worth visiting even without any exhibits.

After having seen the exterior, the museum entrance is a bit discouraging. The halls on the right show archaeological findings: bones, bits and pieces of statues, jewellery, weapons, mosaics and examples of ancient scripts. The explanations are good and make the exhibits a lot more interesting – but they are printed in the local language only. By far the most interesting item is exhibited in the small room on the first floor: the Sarajevo Haggadah. This 14th-century Spanish-Jewish book portrays the world as being round – unheard of at that time. It was taken from Spain to Sarajevo in 1492, disappeared, and reappeared in 1894 when a young boy brought it to the Sarajevo museum.

The Zemaljski Muzej (National Museum)

It was hidden by a Muslim scholar to escape the Holocaust and, in this recent war, taken from the Sarajevo library just weeks before that library went up in flames.

In between the four buildings is the botanic garden with its *stećci* (medieval tombstones). It is a quiet place with benches. The ethnographic exhibition on display in the building on the left is the only part of the museum with good English-language explanations. It tastefully shows all that you would expect from an ethnographic museum, as well as a life-size replica of a rich Ottoman-era family house. ⓐ Zmaja od Bosne 3 ⓣ 033 668 025, 668 026 ⓦ www.zemaljskimuzej.ba ◷ 10.00–17.00 Tues–Fri, 10.00–14.00 Sun. Admission charge

RETAIL THERAPY

Sarajevo is not the place to go on extravagant shopping sprees: there are no large malls or great bargain shopping centres. The best buys are definitely in the small shops that sell locally made goods. Gold and silversmiths in Sarajevo are among the best in southeast Europe, with high-quality jewellery and competitive prices. Leather goods, particularly jackets and bags, are great deals in the leathersmith shops. If it's retail therapy you're looking for, go to the privately owned places to find something unique, high quality and well priced.

Ferhadija and Maršala Tita
The small, privately owned shops on these streets certainly sell the most charming and interesting items in the city centre. There are many brand-name shops (including Miss Selfridge,

Mango, Dorothy Perkins, Sisley and Benetton) along the pedestrian walkway. A neat little open air-market is just after the Eternal Flame on Maršala Tita, through an archway to the left. There are dozens of shops selling all kinds of clothes, music, books and shoes – all at discounted prices.

Skenderija Shopping Centre

If it is raining, or if you would like to see what's on the other side of the river, there is an indoor shopping centre called Skenderija just after the school of fine arts. Many of the shops sell sportswear and footwear. There are also the classic brand-name chains that tend to be more expensive than in the West. Skenderija does house some women's stores with very nice bags and shoes. Like any place in Sarajevo, there are at least a half dozen cafés in the shopping centre. ⓐ Privredni grad, Terezija ⓑ 08.00–19.00 Mon–Sat

Unitic

If you feel like shopping in a luxurious environment, you should go to Unitic, the upper echelon of shopping in Sarajevo. If you are coming from the city centre, you can just walk via the main road, Maršala Tita, and when you come to Marijin Dvor, you will see its two glass towers from there. These twin towers house offices of banks, insurance companies and big international aid organisations, and at ground-floor level there are some congress rooms. The shops sell expensive clothing, jewellery and perfumes. Palma is a great sweet shop on the second floor and there is a good cafeteria-like restaurant on the lower floor. ⓐ Fra Anđela Zvizdovića 1 ⓑ 10.00–21.00 Mon–Sat

TAKING A BREAK

Buybook £ ❶ This is an off-the-beaten-path bookstore and café often frequented by many of Sarajevo's artists and writers. It has a very laid-back atmosphere and the best English book selection in the city. ⓐ Radićeva 4 ⓣ 033 712 010 ⓛ 09.00–22.00 Mon–Sat, 10.00–18.00 Sun

Dva Ribara £ ❷ An old-school Sarajevo café and restaurant. It's perfectly located in the city centre near the National Theatre along the River Miljacka walkway. In the summertime it's a favourite spot for students and a meeting point for the younger crowd. ⓐ Čobanija 2 ⓣ 033 206 525 ⓛ 07.00–22.00

Escobar £ ❸ Just next to the Cathedral on the Ferhadija walkway. The coffee is almost as good as the location, which is an ideal spot for people-watching. ⓐ Fra Grge Martića 4, off Ferhadija ⓣ 033 207 961 ⓛ 08.00–23.00

Galija £ ❹ Just up the road from Dva Ribara. The pizza and service are excellent with a nice shaded terrace to enjoy lunch or a snack. ⓐ Čobanija 20 ⓣ 033 443 350 ⓦ www.galija.ba ⓛ 09.00–23.00 Mon–Sat, 14.00–23.00 Sun

Hot Pizza £ ❺ If you're in a rush or just want to grab a slice of pizza this is the cheapest and most convenient place to do so. They sell only pizza by the slice and soft drinks. ⓐ Ferhadija 5 ⓣ 033 223 393 ⓛ 09.00–00.00 Mon–Sat, 12.00–00.00 Sun ❗ Home delivery available

Kaiser £ ❻ This bakery chain has a great selection of rolls, breads, sandwiches and sweets if you want to grab something and head to the park or to sit outside in nearby Trg Oslobođenja (Liberation Square). ⓐ Ferhadija 6 ⓣ 033 223 393 ⓛ 09.00–00.00 Mon–Sat, 12.00–00.00 Sun

Metropolis £ ❼ Quite possibly the best place in town for its prices, choice, quality and location. It's a local favourite for lunches, snacks, coffee breaks, and for great cakes and ice cream. They also have a tasty breakfast menu, which is hard to come by in Sarajevo. ⓐ Maršala Tita 21 ⓣ 033 203 315 ⓛ 08.00–23.00 Mon–Fri, 09.00–23.00 Sat, 11.00–23.00 Sun

Michelle £ ❽ Located in the epicentre of Sarajevo's pedestrian zone. They serve pizzas, pastas and desserts, both inside and on the other side of the walkway. Finding a seat in the summertime is often a challenge. ⓐ Ferhadija 15 ⓣ 033 444 484 ⓛ 08.00–22.30

Pomodorino £ ❾ Just around the corner from Trg Oslobođenja, this is a great and inexpensive pizza and sandwich spot. They have a seating and standing section or you can take away. There is no outside summer seating. ⓐ Branilaca Sarajeva 51 ⓣ 033 218 810 ⓛ 09.00–23.00 Mon–Sat ⓘ Home delivery available

Cappuccino ££ ❿ Located in the Grbavica quarters, this restaurant along the River Miljacka is a perfect place for a hearty lunch in the shade. The outdoor patio is very popular with a large, shaded area along the river and plenty of room for kids to run around as well. The food and service are top quality and just next door is a great sweet shop for dessert. ⓐ Grbavička 8 ⓣ 033 523 637 ⓦ www.cappuccino.ba ⓛ 09.00–23.00

Mala Kuhinja ££ ⓫ A restaurant that caters to whatever you fancy. The chef will personally wait on you and prepare the combination of your liking with the daily ingredients available. It's a tiny place but well worth making sure you have at least one meal there while in Sarajevo. ⓐ Josipa Stadlera 8 ⓣ 061 144 741 ⓛ 09.00–18.00 Mon–Fri, 09.00–19.00 Sat

AFTER DARK

RESTAURANTS

Avlija £ ⓬ This local favourite, with an earthy and original atmosphere, is an open-air restaurant in the summer and a cosy dining area in the winter. The food and service are excellent. ⓐ Avde Sumbula 2 ⓣ 033 444 483 ⓛ 08.00–22.30 Mon–Sat

Global Foods £ ⓭ It is worth an inexpensive taxi-ride from the city centre to this family-owned restaurant. One of the few places to serve falafel, hummus and other Middle Eastern dishes as well as organic and domestic wines. ⓐ Braće Begića 6 ⓣ 061 274 955 ⓛ 11.00–23.00 Mon–Sat ❗ No credit cards

Hot Wok Café ££ ⓮ Although the menu may not be totally authentic Thai food, Hot Wok is one of the few places in town to get a good taste of Asian cusine. It is also popular for its great cocktails. ⓐ Maršala Tita 12 ⓣ 033 203 322 ⓛ 11.00–23.00 Mon–Fri, 13.00–23.00 Sat

Jež ££ ⓯ Located in an old Austro-Hungarian building near the National Gallery, the food, service and atmosphere here are great and the prices are very reasonable. The menu has a wide array of international dishes. ⓐ Zelenih beretki 14 ⓣ 033 650 312 ⓦ www.jez.ba ◷ 09.00–23.00 Mon–Sat, 17.00–23.00 Sun

Karuso ££ ⓰ Sarajevo's only 'vegetarian' restaurant (they do serve fresh fish and sushi too), this tiny place has fantastic food and is a non-smoking establishment. The menu consists of daily specials that the cook, Sasha, designs himself. The fish is fresh as are all the ingredients. ⓐ Dženetića Čikma, off Pehlivanusa ⓣ 033 444 647 ◷ 12.00–15.00, 18.00–23.00 Mon–Sat

Kibe ££ ⓱ One of the classical national or traditional restaurants in town. It's high up on the hill, so ask for a table with a view of the city and take a taxi to get here. Kibe has a wide range of national dishes: the stews and meat dishes are all excellent. At weekends it's recommended that you book in advance. ⓐ Vrbanjuša 164 ⓣ 033 441 936 ⓦ www.restorankibe.ba ◷ 11.00–23.00 Mon–Sat ❶ No credit cards

Taj Mahal ££ ⓲ A tad off the beaten path, Taj Mahal is Sarajevo's only Indian restaurant. The menu doesn't cover a vast range of Indian meals but the food and service are good. There's a nice vegetarian selection as well. ⓐ Paromlinska 48 ⓣ 061 277 384 ◷ 10.00–23.00 Mon–Sat, 17.00–23.00 Sun ❶ No credit cards

Tavola ££ ⓳ Very near the Eternal Flame on Maršala Tita, this establishment is well-known for its good service and great Italian

food. There's a lengthy selection of dishes and very tasty desserts. ⓐ Maršala Tita 50 ⓣ 033 222 207 ◷ 11.00–23.00 Mon–Fri, 13.30–23.00 Sat & Sun

Plavi Zamak £££ ⓴ The Blue Castle is a favourite spot for the diplomatic corps. The food and service are among the best in town, with a good wine menu. Dalmatian and traditional dishes are served as well as a quality selection of international dishes. The steaks and veal are said to be the best around. ⓐ Zvornička 27 ⓣ 033 657 192 ⓦ www.plavizamak.co.ba ◷ 10.00–23.00 Mon–Sat, 12.00–23.00 Sun ⓡ Trolleybus: direction R. Austrije-Dobrinja (station: Grbavica stadium)

Via del Corso £££ ㉑ Although not located in the most attractive part of town, that's made up for by the classy décor and high-quality food and service. This business-class restaurant serves Italian, French and other international cuisine. ⓐ Kolodvorska 13 ⓣ 033 718 595 ⓦ www.viadelcorso.ba ◷ 10.00–23.00

BARS & CLUBS

Boemi Club Located in the Marijin Dvor quarters, this underground club has many thematic music evenings including flamenco, rave and disco. ⓐ Valtera Perića 16 ⓣ 061 374 350 ◷ 12.00–late Mon–Sat

Central Café *The* 'to see and be seen in' café in Sarajevo. By day it's a bustling outdoor café with highly fashion-conscious patrons. By night it's a popular bar and club, upstairs for socialising, while the basement has a dance floor with live DJs belting out new sounds.

ⓐ Strossmayerova bb ⓣ 033 200 442 ⓦ www.centralcafe.co.ba ⓛ 08.00–03.00

The Club In the basement at the corner of Alipašina and Maršala Tita. It's a more upscale bar with good music, spirits and it's just the bee's knees if you want to stay up late and boogie on down. ⓐ Maršala Tita 7 ⓣ 033 550 550 ⓦ www.theclub.ba ⓛ 10.00–04.00

Kino Bosna One of Sarajevo's classic alternative dives. This grassroots bar attracts the 20- and 30-somethings. It's an alternative crowd with cheap beer and occasional jam sessions. ⓐ Alipašina 19 ⓛ 19.00–00.00 Mon–Sat

Mash This remains one of the best bars in town, just next to the National Theatre; every evening it is packed with a hip and laid-back crowd. There is a live DJ, and it serves excellent food to complement the great atmosphere. ⓐ Branilaca Sarajeva 20/1 ⓣ 062 295 369 ⓛ 08.30–01.00 Mon–Fri, 09.00–03.00 Sat & Sun

Opera Directly across the street from the National Theatre, this relatively new bar has become an overnight hit. Opera is always packed with a young crowd. It serves good cocktails and plays popular music. ⓐ Branilaca Sarajeva 25 ⓣ 061 156 943 ⓦ www.caffebaropera.ba ⓛ 07.00–00.00

Pivnica Sarajevo A super comfy bar with large lounge chairs and couches outside during the summer. The disco bar downstairs has a decent-sized dance floor. The bar serves drinks till quite

late in the evening and there is always a good crowd. ⓐ Maršala Tita br.7 ⓣ 033 555 955 ⓦ www.pivnicasarajevo.ba

Sloga This legendary old bar is actually three floors of fun. The middle floor is a music hall and bar that regularly hosts live music and dancing. The top floor is reminiscent of pre-war Sarajevo – cheap beer, lots of smoke and a very laid-back atmosphere. ⓐ Mehmeda Spahe 20 ⓣ 033 218 811 ⓦ www.cinemas.ba ⓛ 18.30–late

Tito This place conjures up the unique atmosphere of a local bar. And, for an always-welcome dollop of kitsch, the smoky establishment is decorated with Tito memorabilia and is mostly frequented by younger crowds. ⓐ Zmaja od Bosne 5 ⓦ www.caffetito.ba ⓛ 08.00–23.00

Zlatna Ribica The Golden Fish is a quirky but stylish bar that sports great music and a crowd to match it. It's a tiny place with no more than 20 seats in the house but it's a great bar to get the evening started. ⓐ Kaptol 5 ⓣ 061 558 748 ⓛ 07.00–03.00

Ilidža

Ilidža is a suburb just 13 km (8 miles) from the city centre. It is known to have been a settlement long before the sporadic villages formed along the River Miljacka in present-day Sarajevo. One of the most well-known Neolithic sites found on the Balkan peninsula is at Butmir on the outskirts of Ilidža. The Butmir culture is believed to be the northernmost extension of early European civilisation. Ilidža's unique geographical position at the base of Mount Igman lends itself to the vast thermal karst aquifer systems that flow from the high mountain ranges of Igman and Bjelašnica. Since Roman times this settlement has been known for its healing thermal waters, and the Roman presence in the region that lasted for centuries was based in Ilidža. The Ottomans, so impressed with the medicinal qualities of the thermal springs, named it after the Arabic word for 'the cure', *Iladž*. Today this area is much more popular for its parks, thermal springs and close vicinity to the Olympic Mountains rather than the substance of its cultural heritage.

SIGHTS & ATTRACTIONS

The sights and attractions of this Sarajevo suburb are largely nature based. The greatest attraction is the peace and quiet, lovely walking alleys, the plethora of freshwater springs and the healing waters of its thermal spas. For the ski tourist, Ilidža is ideally located just a 20-minute drive from the slopes – and at the end of the day you can return to warm indoor swimming pools and whirlpools.

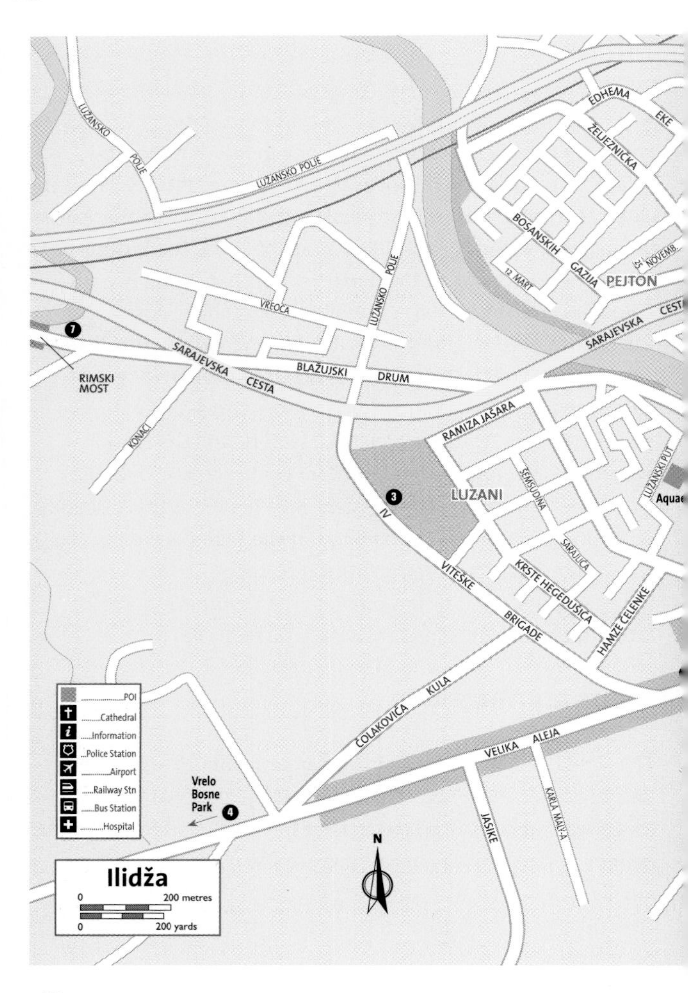
LUŽANSKO
POLJE
LUŽANSKO POLJE
EDHEMA
EKE
ŽELJEZNIČKA
BOSANSKIH
GAZIJA
12 MART
25. NOVEMB.
PEJTON
CESTA
SARAJEVSKA
VREOČA
LUŽANSKO
POLJE
7
RIMSKI
MOST
SARAJEVSKA
CESTA
BLAŽUJSKI
DRUM
RAMIZA JAŠARA
KONACI
ŠEMSUDINA
LUŽANSKI PUT
Aquae
3
LUZANI
IV
VITEŠKE
BRIGADE
SARAJLIĆA
KRSTE HEGEDUŠIĆA
HAMZE ČELENKE
KULA
ČOLAKOVIĆA
VELIKA
ALEJA
KARLA MALY-A
JASIKE
POI
Cathedral
Information
Police Station
Airport
Railway Stn
Bus Station
Hospital
Vrelo
Bosne
Park
4
N
Ilidža
0
200 metres
0
200 yards

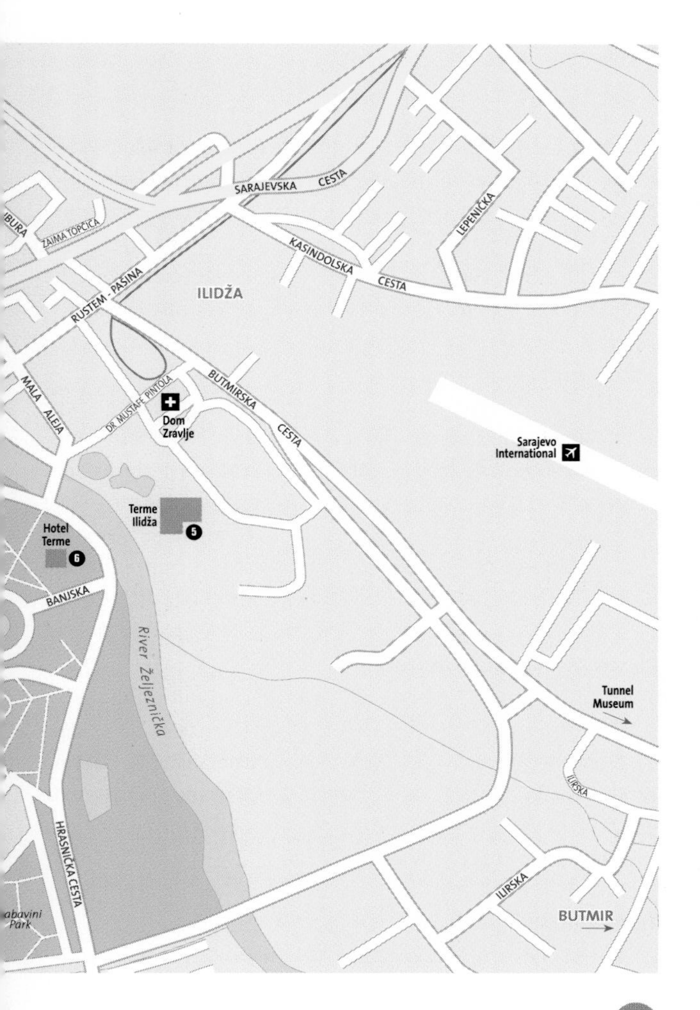
SARAJEVSKA CESTA
ZAIMA TOPČIĆA
KASINDOLSKA CESTA
LEPENIČKA
ILIDŽA
RUSTEM - PAŠINA
BUTMIRSKA CESTA
MALA ALEJA
DR. MUSTAFE PINTOLA
Dom Zravlje
Sarajevo International
Terme Ilidža
5
Hotel Terme
6
BANJSKA
River Željeznička
Tunnel Museum
ILIRSKA
HRASNIČKA CESTA
ILIRSKA
BUTMIR
Park

Aquae S

This archaeological site is what remains of the first-century Roman settlement in Ilidža. This tiny provincial settlement consisted of an administrative centre, residential area and a complex system of thermal spas. Archaeological digs have uncovered Roman ornamental mosaics, pottery, jewellery, and even pipe systems for heating using the thermal waters. The recovered artefacts can be viewed at the Zemaljska Muzej in the city centre but the original ancient ruins are open for viewing. ⓐ Luzanski Put

Hotel Terme

The Austrian-Hungarian empire capitalised on the healing waters and built a hotel complex and thermal centre. Hotel Terme has been renovated and is now probably the best spa in the entire country. The facilities are brand new and offer a wide range of therapies including hydro, physical and recreational. There are two pools and a state-of-the-art physical fitness centre that are accessible to all guests. ⓐ Hrasnička cesta 14 ⓣ 033 772 000

Rimski Most (Roman Bridge)

This 16th-century Ottoman construction was built using the stones from an ancient Roman settlement, hence its name, and is yet another example of the brilliance of Ottoman bridge building. Around the bridge is a popular walking and picnic area. It can be reached most easily from the main road but is a nice walk from the Vrelo Bosne park. ⓐ Blažujski Drum

Terme Ilidža

This modern swimming complex was completed in 2006 and

consists of large indoor and outdoor swimming pools that operate all year round. There is also a café and restaurant, changing room, whirlpool and facilities for children, making it an ideal place for a day trip or a rainy day. ⓐ Mala aleja 40, behind Dom zdravlje ⓣ 033 771 011 ⓦ www.terme-ilidza.ba ⓛ Swimming pool: 09.00–21.00; tropical garden: 08.00–22.00. Admission charge

Velika Aleja

The long tree-lined street is closed to vehicles and is perfect for a jog, walk or bike ride. It is possible to take a horse-and-carriage ride, in an old carriage from the Austro-Hungarian

The 16th-century Ottoman Rimski Most (Roman Bridge)

period, from the top of the avenue. This is the only place in Bosnia and Herzegovina that still practises this tradition. The Austrian nobility were particularly fond of this area and many luxurious villas from that period were built in the area around the sources.

Vrelo Bosne Park (River Bosna Springs)
The park has acres of lush green fields, gushing fresh waters that spring from the surrounding mountains, a large picnic and playing area for children, and two tasty traditional restaurants near one of the largest cascades in the park. It's an ideal way to beat the heat but be aware that weekends are extremely crowded in the park. The springs are accessible by car, foot, bike or horse and carriage.

CULTURE

Butmir (Neolithic settlement)
Evidence of the earliest human settlements in the region were found along the River Željeznička in the small town of Butmir, near Ilidža. This Neolithic settlement dates from 2500 BC and digs have uncovered artefacts and jewellery of highly skilled craftsmen. The Butmir culture is exhibited in the Zemaljski Muzej (see page 86) and although the original settlement can be visited it is poorly organised and difficult to find.

Tunnel Museum
One of the most truly amazing remnants of the resistance to the longest siege in modern European history is the tunnel that

was dug under Sarajevo Airport. For more than three years this tunnel was the only self-sustaining lifeline to the city's wartime population of over 300,000 people. The tunnel was constructed from someone's garage and extended more than 700 m (2,296 ft) under the occupied airport, where it connected to Dobrinja via a labyrinth system of trenches. The museum is run by the family who owns the house where the tunnel began and possesses a wide array of interesting wartime objects. The tunnel is open for viewing but it is now only 20 m (66 ft) deep. You still get a feel for what it must have been like to enter and cross during the heyday of the war. ⓐ Tuneli 1 ⓣ 033 466 885 ⓛ 09.00–18.00. Admission charge

TAKING A BREAK

Dolly Belle £ ❶ Well known for its beautiful summer garden, this is a favourite place for locals to fully implement their café culture. Dolly Belle is located at the beginning of Aleja near the horse-and-carriage station. ⓐ Velika aleja ⓛ 07.00–23.00 Mon–Sat, 08.00–21.00 Sun

Ilidžis £ ❷ A nice café-pizzeria near the beginning of the long pedestrian walkway of Aleja, with a great summer garden. Ideal for lunch or a snack. ⓐ Velika aleja ⓛ 11.00–23.00 Mon–Sat

Restaurant Oaza £ ❸ Located at the entrance to the bungalow and camping facility Oaza. The outdoor terrace is quiet and peaceful with affordable lunches and snacks. Like most places in Sarajevo, you are most welcome to sit for a coffee or lemonade too. ⓐ IV Viteške Brigade 3 ⓣ 033 636 140 ⓛ 12.00–00.00 Mon–Sat

Restaurant Vrelo Bosne £ ❹ While visiting the Vrelo Bosne Park, this lovely restaurant is located near one of the larger cascades. All paths within the park lead to this area, making it very easy to find. The meat and trout dishes are the house specialities and you are free to sit and just have a coffee as well. ⓐ Vrelo Bosne ⓑ 10.00–23.00

Terme Ilidža £ ❺ The tropical garden restaurant and café is a great place for a lunch break or a coffee at any time of year. ⓐ Mala aleja 40 ⓣ 033 771 011 ⓦ www.terme-ilidza.ba ⓑ 08.30–22.30

AFTER DARK

Hotel Terme ££ ❻ The restaurant here is also open to non-guests. The food, largely traditional meat dishes, is well prepared and the service is excellent. They have a nice regional wine selection and quiet outdoor café for an after-dinner drink. ⓐ Hrasnička cesta 14 ⓣ 033 772 000 ⓑ 07.00–23.00

Rimski Most ££ ❼ Located on the River Željeznička near the Roman Bridge, this restaurant serves excellent traditional meals, particularly veal. The service is good and during the high season the summer garden is cool and refreshing. ⓐ Blažujski Drum bb ⓣ 033 761 180, 761 190 ⓦ www.hotel-rimskimost.com ⓑ 07.00–22.00

Bjelašnica, site of the XIV Winter Olympics

OUT OF TOWN
trips

The Olympic Mountains

One of the beauties of skiing or hiking in Sarajevo is the proximity of the mountains to the city centre. The XIV Winter Olympic Games was one of the largest and most successful of its time. Although some of the infrastructure was destroyed during the war, much of that has been reconstructed making Sarajevo's Olympic Mountains one of the most attractive and inexpensive ski centres in southeast Europe. There aren't any high-tech modern lifts or posh alpine villas, but no one can dispute the quality of the slopes, snow and fun to be had skiing on these Olympic Mountains.

Jahorina is the largest ski centre in the country with dozens of hotels and private accommodation on the mountain. Bjelašnica is more limited, as much of the accommodation was destroyed during the conflict. The close vicinity of the city, however, gives a ski holiday an interesting twist. As the sun sets at around 16.00 in the winter, it's a great opportunity to get the best of both worlds and pop into the city for dinner, a film or a play, or just bar-hop before hitting the slopes the next morning.

In terms of summer activities, Bjelašnica Mountain is a nature lover's paradise. There is a great selection of walking, hiking, biking and highland village trips. Lukomir medieval village is certainly the highlight of Bjelašnica's ancient alpine villages, offering a peek into old world Europe's ancient past. Jahorina and Igman are also nice areas for picnics or walking, with a limited number of marked trails.

Green Visions (see page 35) ecotourism group regularly runs biking, hiking, rafting and village trips throughout the area all

A ski lift on Jahorina Mountain

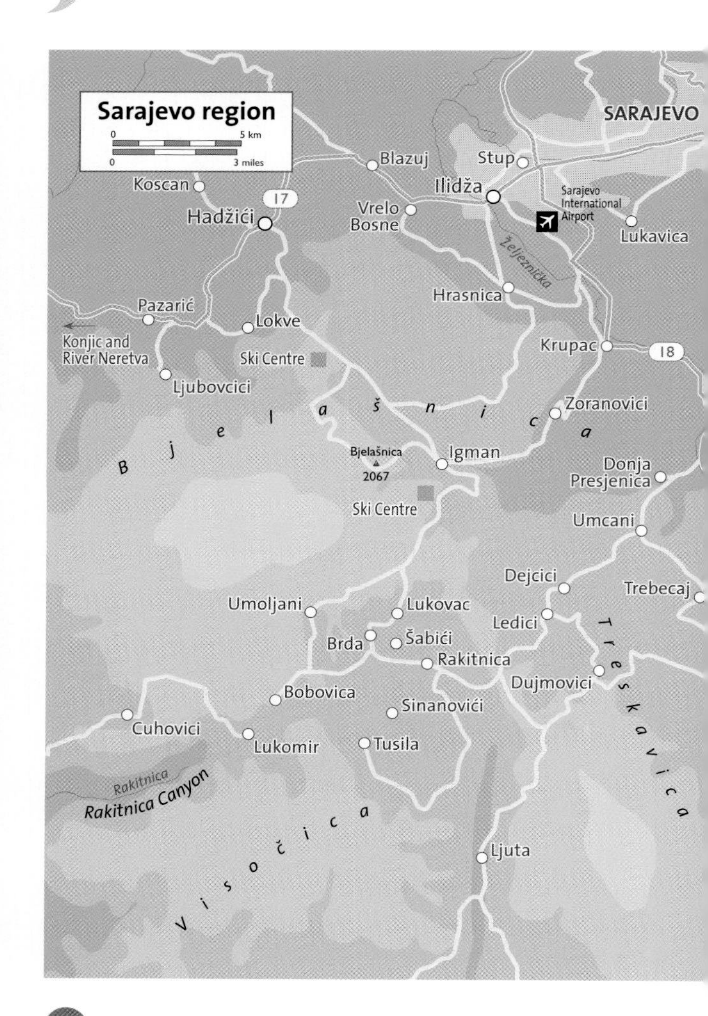
Sarajevo region
0
5 km
0
3 miles
SARAJEVO
Blazuj
Stup
Ilidža
Koscan
17
Hadžići
Vrelo
Bosne
Sarajevo
International
Airport
Lukavica
Željeznička
Hrasnica
Pazarić
Lokve
Konjic and
River Neretva
Ski Centre
Krupac
18
Ljubovcici
Bjelašnica
Zoranovici
Bjelašnica
2067
Igman
Donja
Presjenica
Ski Centre
Umcani
Dejcici
Trebecaj
Umoljani
Lukovac
Ledici
Brda
Šabići
Rakitnica
Treskavica
Dujmovici
Bobovica
Sinanovići
Cuhovici
Lukomir
Tusila
Rakitnica
Rakitnica Canyon
Visočica
Ljuta

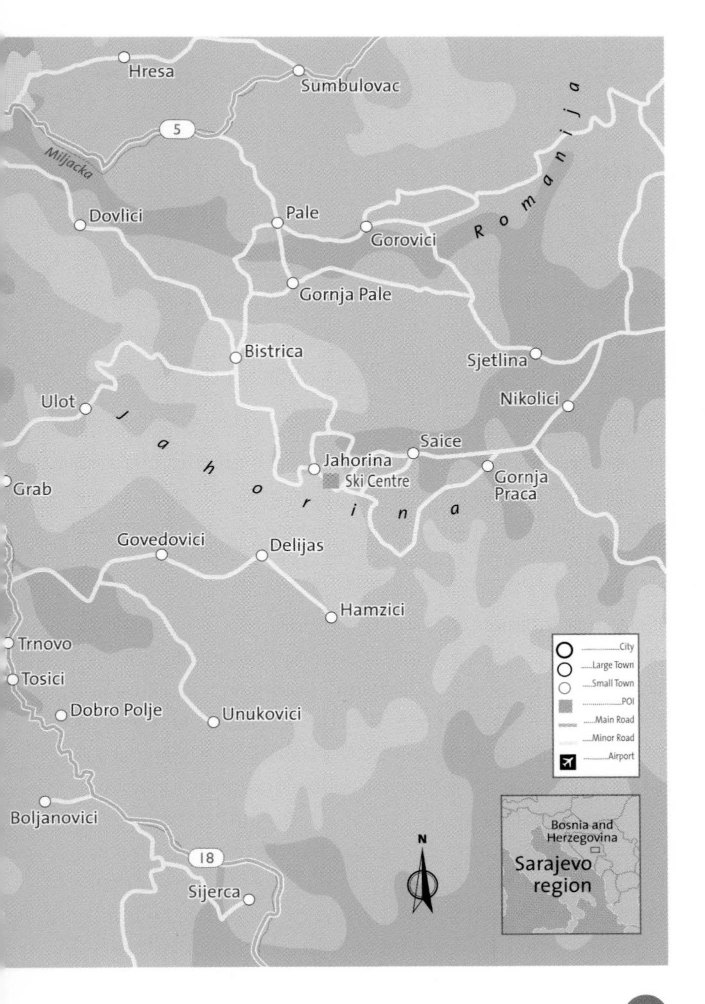
Hresa
Sumbulovac
5
Miljacka
Romanija
Dovlici
Pale
Gorovici
Gornja Pale
Bistrica
Sjetlina
Nikolici
Ulot
Jahorina
Saice
Jahorina
Ski Centre
Gornja Praca
Grab
Govedovici
Delijas
Hamzici
Trnovo
Tosici
Dobro Polje
Unukovici
City
Large Town
Small Town
POI
Main Road
Minor Road
Airport
Boljanovici
Bosnia and Herzegovina
Sarajevo region
N
18
Sijerca

summer long. They provide professionally run day and weekend trips with transport, guides, lunch and all necessary safety equipment on river rafting excursions.

GETTING THERE

Jahorina

This is reachable via the Sarajevo–Pale road, which is a 20 minute drive from the old town and another 15 minutes from Pale. The roads are well marked but do expect the occasional Cyrillic alphabet sign once you get closer to Jahorina. During the winter months there is a bus that leaves from the Zemaljski Muzej between 08.00 and 09.00. The buses are sometimes unreliable so best to ask the receptionist at your accommodation to make a phone call or ask at the tourist information centre in Sarajevo. The return buses usually depart between 16.00 and 17.00; ask the driver on the outbound journey, as return times can vary.

Bjelašnica & Igman

During the spring and summer the only consistent public transport to Bjelašnica and Igman mountains is via Ilidža and Hadžići. There are minibuses that travel twice daily from Ilidža to Igman–Bjelašnica–Sinanovići via Hadžići. The cost is around 2 KM. During the winter months public transport is provided from the Zemaljski Muzej (National Museum); it leaves between 08.00 and 09.00 and returns after dark between 16.00 and 17.00. Some hotels provide private transport to the slopes and the tourist information centre has regular updates on transport to the mountain. Bjelašnica is only a 25-minute drive from the

Ancient medieval tombstone on a highland path

city centre on the quickest route. The Ilidža–Hadžići route is considerably longer.

To avoid relying on local buses, which can have unpredictable or inconvenient times, you may be best off hiring a car or taxi (see page 58) or taking a tour (see page 35). If you are on a very tight budget and do decide to brave the buses, make sure you fully understand the return times and destinations.

SIGHTS & ATTRACTIONS

Jahorina Ski Centre

The country's largest ski centre, Jahorina managed to escape most of the horrors of the war and has since expanded greatly with weekend homes, boutique hotels, and an impressive range of traditional restaurants and shops to serve the many skiers who come from all over the region. The centre is only 30 km (19 miles) east of Sarajevo – it is an easy day trip from the city, or you could spend a few nights at one of Jahorina's many hotels (there are over 15 to choose from). The skiing on Jahorina is less challenging than on Bjelašnica, but there are many more ski trails and good snow tends to last longer.

Jahorina's highest peak is 1,910 m (6,266 ft) with the ski lift reaching almost to the top. The long trails wind through an impressive maze of beautiful pine forests that dominate Jahorina up to about 1,600 m (5,250 ft). The ski lifts are a bit out of date, but get you where you want to go nonetheless. Snowboarding is becoming quite popular here, with plenty of room on the slopes for boarders. There are several places where you can hire ski equipment, and you can get information on skiing lessons at

The verdant meadows of Bjelašnica in summertime

the ski ticket booth. For more general information on Jahorina, visit www.oc-jahorina.com

Bjelašnica & Igman Ski Centres

The war ruthlessly brought these two Olympic Centres to their knees – both were razed to the ground during the fighting that raged from 1992–95. Bjelašnica, home to the men's slalom and Bosnia's steepest and toughest ski mountain, has made a comeback over the past few years; significant construction has taken place, and future plans include expanding the ski routes to nearly three times the current capacity. There are now apartments to rent and a bigger choice of dining facilities since these were built. Equipment is available to hire at several locations that are clearly marked.

Igman is the smallest of the Olympic venues. It is a great place for beginners or children, with extra activities such as horse and sleigh rides available. Due to the limited accommodation and the general lack of nightlife at Igman, most visitors choose to stay in Sarajevo and visit Igman during the day to ski.

Highland areas

The highlands of Bjelašnica are an amazing place to visit and there is regular transport to the area. This is a place where you can dip into old-world Europe and experience some of the country's most stunning natural beauty. However, it should be noted that a large number of live mines and other explosive weapons have been left behind from the war in Bosnia and Herzegovina. The main affected areas may be dotted with a few official warning signs, but if you do plan to visit the mountains without the help of a local guide or through an organised tour, it is necessary to be adequately informed about the possible dangers. Refer to ⓦ www.bhmac.org for helpful information when planning your hiking or biking venture.

Lukomir Medieval Village

This remote highland village has become a highlight for many visitors. Perched high in the alpine meadows of the Bjelašnica mountains' eastern border, this medieval village is a window to Europe's ancient past. Traditional lifestyles from well before the arrival of the Ottomans in the 15th century have been preserved, and many women still wear the handmade attire that is characteristic of the mountain tribes of the Central Dinaric Alps. The homes maintain their rustic design, with hand-carved stone walls, steep wood shingle roofs, and the unique lack of a chimney. The smoke from the wood burner in each house goes directly into the attic area, and acts a sealant and insulator for the long and brutal winters.

There are great hiking trails to and from the village. Due to its remoteness, it is recommended that you hire a guide or go with a travel agency that operates regular tours to this highland wonder.

Rakitnica Canyon

Rakitnika Canyon is an inspiring sight that locals boast is one of southeastern Europe's most unexplored canyons. Access to the canyon is limited and can be dangerous, so it is highly recommended that you go with a guide. This geomorphological phenomenon is a result of an ancient rift in the karst topography that now separates Bjelašnica from the Visocica mountain. This

rift created the area's only southern water flow, via the Neretva river to the Adriatic Sea basin, instead of the normal northern flow to the Black Sea. The entire length of this 26 km (16 mile) canyon is home to endemic species of flora and is teeming with wildlife.

Šabići

Šabići village, 1,160 m (3,806 ft) above sea level, nestles in the upper valley of the River Rakitnica, yet is only 15 minutes from Sarajevo. This is a new location for a students' lodge, as well as a mountaineer lodge, making it one of the easier places to find accommodation on your own. Being the main village in the region, most of the necessary facilities are based here, including a school and a medical clinic.

Umoljani

This tiny village of some 20-odd homes was completely destroyed in the early 1990s, but is becoming increasingly popular with nature lovers. Although the traditional architecture of the village has largely disappeared, the traditional lifestyles haven't. The locals are mainly shepherds, with large flocks of sheep dotting the mountainside. Small, organic agricultural concerns are becoming more and more popular, with many Sarajevans visiting the area regularly to buy veggies and dine at the two restaurants that serve home-made meals.

With relatively easy access from Sarajevo, Umoljani has become a base for a wide range of hiking tours. You can visit old water mills that are still used to produce flour, and the valley of

Living history at Lukomir Medieval Village

Studeni Polje has a serpentine stream that falls 400 m (1,312 ft) into Rakitnica Canyon. From here, it is possible to hike all the way to Lukomir and loop back round to Umoljani in one day. Trails are not well marked, so it is recommended that you go with a guide.

Rafting the River Neretva
The southern slopes of Bjelašnica Mountain near the town of Konjic end at the River Neretva. This crystal-clear mountain river has become one of the most popular whitewater rafting destinations in southeast Europe. The long and fun journey stretches over 28 km (16 miles) and takes an estimated 4–6 hours to raft. The Neretva is a Class 2 river, making it safe for children as well. The minimum age limit is ten years old. This deep river canyon has stunning scenery and, to make the trip even more amazing, the river water is so clean it's potable for most of the trip.

CULTURE

The most fascinating aspect of Bjelašnica Mountain is certainly the highland village culture that has flourished here for thousands of years. Not too long ago the highlanders practised a semi-nomadic lifestyle, criss-crossing the vast mountain range with their flocks. Many villages are still reliant on this lifestyle but the trans-migratory culture was drastically hindered during the war when many of the villages were torched. Some villages did survive the war, however, and several more have been rebuilt in the old style.

Villagers in traditional Bosnian attire

But, as is the case in Sarajevo, the people are the true gem of the Bjelašnica Mountain range. The local villagers are extremely kind and will welcome any visitor who comes their way. Although very poor, they will always treat you as a member of the family and provide you with food and drink. Their lifestyles are totally dependent on their relationship to the land. Most things they have are produced within their own communities. The influences of the modern world have certainly touched the highland populations, but rest assured that this area is one of the last remaining of its kind in Europe.

RETAIL THERAPY

There are no shopping areas within the ski centres or throughout the mountain range. Jahorina does have several shops selling equipment, clothes and ski necessities just next to Hotel Košuta. For genuine handmade wool products like socks, scarves and jumpers, the knitting talent of the highlanders is unmatched. Some of the handicrafts may seem a bit expensive, but keep in mind the process. Traditional highlander wool spinning is an A–Z handmade process. The sheep are hand-sheared, the wool is then hand-washed and spun, dyed and only then does the knitting process begin. Due to the harsh weather conditions the quality is superb – it has to be. Most villages listed under sights and attractions will have wool products available for sale. There are no 'shops' per se but the village women are likely to approach any foreigners who come for a visit. Also ask your guide where the best place may be to purchase these sturdy and beautiful highland products.

TAKING A BREAK

BJELAŠNICA

Aroma £ Very much a local dive, this minimalist establishment offers nothing fancy but serves high-quality and good-value local dishes. The outside terrace is the best choice, as establishments of this sort are always accompanied by heavy smoking. Babin do bb 033 414 100 08.00–20.00

Restaurant Benetton £ This is the most convenient place for a quick bite to eat or a hot cup of tea or coffee whilst skiing on Bjelašnica. The service isn't the best, but being located just at the base of the piste makes up for it. Babin do bb 061 548 723 08.00–19.00

Restaurant Planinska Kuća £ This log cabin restaurant has become a Bjelašnica landmark which serves eco-sourced, local food. Most famous for its Dutch oven pies made with meat, cheese, spinach and potatoes; they are usually accompanied by fresh yoghurt. Babin do bb 033 130 352 10.00–20.00 Nov–Feb, 07.00–19.00 Mar–Oct

IGMAN

Mražište £ Currently the only restaurant/café facility near the Igman ski slopes. The restaurant largely serves a traditional menu, with excellent veal and stews. Igman Ski Centre 033 412 002 Times vary, winter only

AFTER DARK

JAHORINA

Peggy £ Also a local favourite serving very reasonably priced traditional foods. Its *ćevapi* (spicy sausage) is said to be the best in Jahorina. By night it's a dance club with great music and cheap beer. ⓐ Near hotel Sator ⓣ 057 270 210 ⓦ www.peggy-jahorina.com

Termag £ This hotel is also known for its great restaurant. Serving both international and local cuisine, you can't go wrong here. The food and service are excellent. ⓐ Poljice ⓣ 057 272 100, 270 422 ⓦ www.termaghotel.com ⓛ 06.00–00.00

BJELAŠNICA

Srebrna Lisica ££ A restaurant on Bjelašnica just next to Hotel Maršal (see page 124). The 'silver fox' in translation has a dynamic menu, good wine list, and excellent décor. ⓐ Babin do 3 ⓣ 033 579 000

ACCOMMODATION

JAHORINA

Hotel Košuta ££ This socialist-era hotel offers good, mid-range skiing accommodation on Jahorina. The rooms are comfortable and clean, and the restaurant prides itself on being one of the best on the mountain. They often have live Serbian folk music as well. ⓐ Jahorina bb ⓣ 057 270 401

Hotel Kristal ££ One of the more chic places on Jahorina. Service is certainly more western-style, as is the décor. It is conveniently located near one of the ski lifts, making quick lunch breaks an easy affair. ⓐ Jahorina bb ⓣ 057 226 574, 226 725

Hotel Nebojša ££ This is one of Jahorina's newer, medium-sized hotels. Well known for its ski garden, which attracts not only the hotel's guests but also a large following of skiers who enjoy it while pausing for lunch. The rooms are spacious, the décor

Snow-covered Termag ski-resort hotel and restaurant

tasteful, and the food and service are excellent. ⓐ Jahorina bb ⓣ 057 270 500 ⓦ www.hotel-nebojsa.com

Hotel Termag ££ Termag is certainly one of the nicest Alpine ski lodges in the country. Aside from its impressive exterior and interior design, Termag offers excellent cuisine and service. The rooms are spacious and cosy. It is located in the heart of the Jahorina Ski Centre with ski lifts very close to the hotel. ⓐ Poljice bb ⓣ 057 272 100, 270 422 ⓦ www.termaghotel.com

BJELAŠNICA

Hotel Maršal ££ Currently the Bjelašnica Ski Centre's only hotel. Although something of an eyesore from the outside, the rooms and food are of good quality. Marsal is located only a few hundred metres from the main ski lift. In the off season, though, the hotel tends to be a bit of a ghost town. ⓐ Babin do I ⓣ 033 279 100 ⓦ www.hotel-marsal.ba

Elegant tourist information office

PRACTICAL
information

Directory

GETTING THERE

By air

Travel by air to Sarajevo is still on the expensive side; none of the cheap airlines serve the city as yet. The main connection hubs for other means of air travel to Bosnia and Herzegovina's capital are Croatia Airlines via Zagreb and Austrian Airlines via Vienna.

The only cheap airlines in the region are easyJet, Germanwings, and Wizzair: they all fly into Croatia during the high season from May to late October. Cheap flights destinations are Dubrovnik, Split and Zagreb. All of these Croatian destinations are well connected to Sarajevo via bus or train.

Alitalia t 0871 424 1424 w www.alitalia.co.uk
Austrian Airlines t 020 7766 0300 w www.aua.com/uk
Croatia Airlines t 020 8563 0022 w www.croatiaairlines.hr
Lufthansa t 0870 8377 747 w www.lufthansa.com

Many people are aware that air travel emits CO_2, which contributes to climate change. You may be interested in the possibility of lessening the environmental impact of your flight through the charity **Climate Care** (w www.climatecare.org), which offsets your CO_2 by funding environmental projects around the world.

By rail

There are direct daily trains to Sarajevo from three main destinations: Ploče on the Croatian coast, Zagreb and Budapest. With Zagreb and Budapest well linked to the European railway system it is an easy way to get to Sarajevo for considerably less than an expensive airfare. The trains in this part of the world are rather old and occasionally shabby, but nonetheless are a decent means of travel. Train travel is time-consuming, with trains from Zagreb to Sarajevo taking at least nine hours and from Budapest

Sarajevo Train Station, built during the Communist era

over ten hours. Bosnia and Herzegovina is a member of the InterRail pass system so, if you are travelling in the region, this is a cost-effective way to travel. Check out the main InterRail website for travel from the UK and around Europe. For times see the *Thomas Cook European Rail Timetable*.

The southernmost point to travel by train along the Croatian Coast is to Ploče. From Ploče the train heads east and enters Bosnia and Herzegovina around Metković and travels to Sarajevo via Mostar. If you plan on taking a Eurorail or InterRail pass, keep in mind that there are no direct connections from Dubrovnik. See these websites for more details.

InterRail UK ⓣ 08700 84 14 11 ⓦ www.interrail.com
RailEurope UK ⓣ 0870 584 8848 ⓦ www.raileurope.co.uk
Thomas Cook European Rail Timetable ⓣ UK: (01733) 416 477, USA: 1 800 322 3834 ⓦ www.thomascookpublishing.com

By road

Bus travel in southeast Europe is not only very affordable but it enjoys by far the best network of travel connections in every direction. Eurolines in co-operation with Centrotrans Sarajevo offers return tickets to London once a week. Bus travel is extremely long, often lasting more than 36 hours to Sarajevo from the UK. There is the likelihood of finding a less expensive option via a cheap air flight to the region and then taking a bus to Sarajevo.

Centrotrans ⓦ www.centrotrans.ba
Eurolines ⓣ 0870 514 3219 ⓦ www.eurolines.co.uk

If you've decided on the long haul from the UK and you're driving yourself, the quickest and most travelled route is via Brussels, Cologne, Frankfurt, Salzburg, Graz and Zagreb. It's wiser to take the motorway from Zagreb to Slavonski Brod and make the border crossing there. After crossing into Bosnia the motorway disappears and you will have two-lane roads all the way to Sarajevo. If coming from the Croatian coast there are three practical entry points: 1. Dubrovnik via Trebinje to Stolac, Mostar and the M17 to Sarajevo; 2. Metković is the main border crossing in the southern region – from Metković it is a straight shoot to Mostar on the M17 direct on to Sarajevo; 3. from the Split area to Sinj and crossing at Kamensko. From Kamensko take the main road to Livno, Kupres, Bugojno, Travnik and Sarajevo. It is a long but extremely beautiful road.

Parking in Sarajevo is limited but there are parking lots with attendants throughout the city. Some hotels offer adequate parking; when making reservations in advance it's a good idea to ask the receptionist about the availability of parking.

Roads in Bosnia and Herzegovina are very winding with only a few dozen kilometres of proper motorway. The roads are in fairly good condition but be forewarned of aggressive drivers making nerve-racking passes on bends.

ENTRY FORMALITIES

For holders of valid passports from the UK, Republic of Ireland, all other EU countries, USA, Canada and Australia and New Zealand, no visa is required for stays up to 90 days. Holders of South African passports must obtain visas at the Bosnian embassies in either London or Tripoli (Libya). For South African nationals already in the region it is possible to obtain a visa from the Embassy of Bosnia and Herzegovina in Zagreb, Belgrade or Ljubljana. For any extended stays it is easiest to simply cross the border into Croatia, Montenegro or Serbia and re-enter. For Western travellers, border control in Bosnia and Herzegovina is particularly lax. For those requiring visas the cost for a single entry tourist or business visa is currently £20, £36 for a multiple entry for up to 90 days and £45 for multiple entry for more than 90 days. Visa applications usually take three weeks to process as all applications are sent to and verified in Sarajevo. For any further information contact the **Embassy of Bosnia & Herzegovina in the UK** (ⓐ 5–7 Lexham Gardens, London W8 5JJ ⓣ 020 7373 0867 ⓦ www.bhembassy.co.uk ⓛ 09.00–17.00 Mon–Fri (consular section, personal callers)).

Customs restrictions basically follow EU regulations. The limit for cigarettes is 200 and alcohol is 2 l (½ gal).

MONEY

The official unit of currency in Bosnia and Herzegovina is the konvertebilna marka (convertible mark) or KM. On international exchanges it is labelled BAM. This currency is fixed to the euro at 1.95. Notes come in 1, 5, 10, 20, 50, 100 and 200 denominations. Euros are readily accepted in most places in Sarajevo although public institutions such as the post office and public transport accept only local currency. Most cafés, bars, restaurants and places of business will exchange euros for you. All of the banks have exchange offices throughout the city. There aren't many bureaux de change as found in the West; most exchanges are done by banks and the post office.

ATMs are found throughout the city with English options available on all of them. Traveller's cheques can be exchanged only in banks. Sarajevo basically has a cash-only economy. Credit cards are accepted in some venues, but be prepared for many places, even hotels, not to accept payment by credit card. Visa and MasterCard are the most commonly used and accepted cards in the city.

HEALTH, SAFETY & CRIME

Most Westerners would find medical care in the public institutions of Sarajevo to be under par at best. There are two hospitals (*bolnica*) in Sarajevo. Both have adequate facilities for emergencies. A basic medical clinic (called *Dom zdravlja*) can offer medical care for non-emergencies. Most travellers prefer private clinics (*privatna klinika* or *ordinacija*) where the level of health care is better. Pharmacies (*apoteka*) are located in each neighbourhood of Sarajevo and are usually open from 08.00–19.00 with several all-night pharmacies open for emergencies. Health insurance is a complicated issue and although there are agreements with EU countries you will most likely have to pay cash and look for reimbursement from your insurance company. The cost of medical care is considerably less than in all Western countries. It is best to check with your insurance company on their policy before travelling to Bosnia and Herzegovina.

Sarajevo, despite the horrible images of the war from over a decade ago, is quite a safe city. Violent crime is virtually non-existent and, although it is always wise to use precautions if wandering late at night, most crime is limited to pickpocketing on trams, trolleybuses and in crowded pedestrian areas. Single women should always take precautions when travelling. Be advised that some men may interpret or confuse friendliness with a willingness for something more. Use your guard and be assertive if men come on too strong.

OPENING HOURS

Most shops are open 08.00–20.00 Monday to Saturday. During the high season many shops will remain open until 22.00, especially in the old town. Many of the handicraft shops, however, will close earlier. Food stores and supermarkets are open until 22.00. There are several 24-hour shops that are marked '0–24'. These late-night shops usually have a small window open where you can tell the clerk what you would like. It is most likely you cannot enter the premises after 00.00. Open-air markets usually open a bit earlier, at 07.00, and remain open often till nightfall in the summer months, but officially until 19.00. Banks are generally open 08.00–20.00. Banking hours are 08.00–20.00 Monday to Friday, 09.00–14.00 Saturday. Public institutions close rather early, some at 15.00 but most at 16.00.

TOILETS

Most places in Sarajevo do not require you to be a 'paying customer' to use the toilet facilities; it is best to ask but it is a rarity for a foreigner to be rejected. Toilets are almost exclusively labelled 'WC' or 'Toilet' so no confusion as to where to go. The toilets will be labelled 'Ž' for *ženski* (female) and 'M' for *muški* (male). In many of the older buildings the toilet will simply be a hole in the ground, usually with no toilet paper. Look for newer establishments for modern facilities. A few places will charge a small fee for using the toilet. Public toilets in Sarajevo are few and far between.

CHILDREN

The entire former Yugoslavia is very child-friendly, with Sarajevo being no different. With few exceptions, children are welcome in restaurants and cafés. Most cafés and restaurants will go out of their way to provide special orders for children as well. There aren't many areas specifically designed for children. At-Mejdan in the old town (see page 61) is a small park with children's rides. The **Sarajevo Zoo** (@ Patriotske Lige), does not have many exotic animals but is a very nice place for children. There is a playground as well as a petting zoo. The admission charge is only 1 KM for kids. The Terme Ilidža (see page 100) has excellent swimming facilities for children and the Vrelo Bosne park in Ilidža is a wonderful place for children to run around and play. The Sarajevo Film Festival in late-August has a kids' film fest for every night of the festival at the Skenderija shopping centre.

COMMUNICATIONS

Internet

Only a limited number of hotels have internet connection for guests but there are plenty of internet cafés around town. The newer places will have ADSL quick connections while some will still be on dial-up – it's best to ask before buying internet credit. **Internet Club Click** is on Kundurdžiluk street in the old town.

Telephones

Public phones, called *govornica*, use phone cards that can be purchased at any post office or the small kiosks around town. Phone cards come in 10, 20 or 50 KM. From a payphone, simply dial the six-digit number within the Sarajevo region. For Jahorina, dial 057 first then the six-digit number. Local assistance is (t) 1182 but they are unlikely to speak English. If you are calling from a mobile phone within Bosnia and Herzegovina with a local SIM card, you must use the full prefix (061, 062, 063, 065) followed by the number.

TELEPHONING BOSNIA & HERZEGOVINA

Landline phones:

Dialling code + 387

Dialling code for Sarajevo (0)33

Mobile phones:

+ 387 61 + number

+ 387 62 + number

+ 387 63 + number

+ 387 65 + number

depending on which network the person is using

TELEPHONING ABROAD

00 + country code + local number

Dialling codes:

Australia 61

Canada 1

Ireland 353

New Zealand 64

South Africa 27

UK 44

USA 1

Mobile phones from North America do not work in Bosnia. Other European networks are rather expensive in Sarajevo. Buying a local SIM card will cost only 50 KM for a phone number and 10 KM worth of credit. BH Telekom is the local phone company and all post offices and many kiosks sell new phone cards. Instructions are provided in English.

Post office

Stamps (*marka*, sing. *marke*, pl.) can only be bought at the post office. Postcards to the UK cost around 1 KM and about double that for countries further afield. The post within Europe takes approximately one week and to North America, around two weeks. The post office is consistently inconsistent with its timing. Sending packages to any destination is quite expensive, including any of the Western couriers such as DHL and FedEx.

ELECTRICITY

Bosnia uses 220 V and the standard continental Europe two-pin plugs. It is very difficult to find an adaptor in Sarajevo for UK or US plugs.

TRAVELLERS WITH DISABILITIES

Although the number of people with disabilities drastically increased as a result of the war, assistance or facilities for people with disabilities is practically nonexistent. Just recently the pavements of Sarajevo were installed with ramps for wheelchairs, but even this is not consistently done throughout the city.

TOURIST INFORMATION

There is only one **tourism information centre** (TIC ⓐ Zelenih beretki 22A ⓣ 033 220 724, 220 721 ⓦ www.sarajevo-tourism.com ⓑ 09.00–21.00 Mon–Fri, 09.00–20.00 Sat & Sun, June–Sept; 09.00–21.00 Mon–Fri, 09.00–16.00 Sat, Oct–May) in Sarajevo. It is located in the old town. The staff are very helpful and will do everything they can to assist. There is a monthly events calendar distributed free of charge and other brochures are available at the TIC.

Useful websites

www.bhtourism.ba is the official website of Bosnia and Herzegovina. Here you will find fairly detailed information on hotels, attractions and tour operators.
www.greenvisions.ba is a Sarajevo-based ecotourism operator that organises hikes, biking and rafting throughout the Sarajevo area. They are also a local partner of UK travel agencies Exodus and Regents Holidays.
www.sarajevo-tourism.com is Canton Sarajevo's tourism website. There is a complete list of hotels, bars, and listings for the cultural life in Sarajevo.
www.visitbosnia.ba is a website dedicated to responsible and green tourism. Here you'll find listings for family-owned establishments and ways to support local communities and artists when travelling in Bosnia and Herzegovina.

BACKGROUND READING

Bridge Over the Drina by Ivo Andrić. The Nobel Prize-winning author's novel about the ethnic tensions of Ottoman Bosnia.

Hearts Grown Brutal by Roger Cohen. A saga of the siege of Sarajevo told through the lives of four families.
Bosnia, A Short History by Noel Malcolm. A clear and concise account of this Balkan nation's turbulent history.
Sarajevo Marlboro by Miljenko Jergović. A story of everyday life in Sarajevo by one of the city's most famous and successful writers.
Fighting for Peace by General Sir Michael Rose. A striking depiction of the war in Bosnia from the eyes of a British UN general.

Emergencies

EMERGENCY TELEPHONE NUMBERS

Ambulance ⓣ 124

Fire ⓣ 123

Police ⓣ 122

MEDICAL SERVICES

Hospitals and emergency centre

At both hospitals you can find English-speaking doctors and medical staff. It is best to go to Koševo Medical Centre where they have modern facilities.

Koševo Medical Centre ⓐ Bolnička 25 ⓣ 033 297 000

State Hospital ⓐ Kranjčevićeva 12 ⓣ 033 285 100

Private medical clinic

Poliklinika Sanasa This private clinic is located in the Grbavička neighbourhood of the city centre. ⓐ Grbavička 74 ⓣ 033 661 841 ⓔ poliklinikasanasa@smartnet.ba ⓛ 09.00–17.00 Mon–Fri, 09.00–14.00 Sat

Dentist

Ordanicija Konjhodžić The dentist is a professor at the faculty and speaks fluent English. ⓐ Bolnička 5 ⓣ 033 229 749, 061 487 290 ⓛ 15.00–20.00 Mon–Fri

POLICE

There are a great number of police officers in Sarajevo and many of them are on foot patrol. Always try to contact them first in an

EMERGENCY PHRASES

Help!	**Fire!**	**Stop!**
Upomoć!	Pozar!	Stanite!
Oopoh-mohtch!	*Poh djar!*	*Stah-nee-teh!*
Police!	**I need a doctor**	
Policiju!	Treba mi doktor	
Poh-lee-tsee-yoo!	*Treh-bah mee dohk-tohr*	

emergency – quite often when they discover a foreigner is involved they will call an English-speaking officer to the scene. However, when calling the emergency numbers you will not always find an English speaker.

EMBASSIES & CONSULATES

Canada ⓐ 4 Grbavička, Sarajevo ⓣ 033 222 033
ⓔ sjevo@dfait-maeci-gc.ca ⓛ 09.00–16.00 Mon–Fri
USA ⓐ Alipašina 43, Sarajevo ⓣ 033 445 700
ⓦ www.sarajevo.usembassy.gov ⓛ 08.00–11.30 Tues & Thur, 10.00–15.30 Mon, Wed & Fri
UK ⓐ Tina Ujevića 8, Sarajevo ⓣ 033 282 200
ⓦ www.britishembassy.gov.uk ⓛ 08.30–17.00 Mon–Thur, 08.30–14.30 Fri

Editorial/project management: Lisa Plumridge
Copy editor: Paul Hines
Layout/DTP: Alison Rayner
Proofreader: Judy Johnson

The publishers would like to thank the following individuals and organisations for supplying their copyright photographs for this book: BigStockPhoto.com (Zoran Jagrovic, pages 107 & 123; Amra Pasic, pages 24–5 & 105); Munever Salihovic, pages 17, 19, 45, 47, 82, 84, 87 & 125; Sarajevo Film Festival, page 15; Shock/Fotolia.com, pages 23 & 67; Tourism Association of Bosnia and Herzegovina, pages 7 & 59; Sebastien Venuat, pages 9, 11, 21, 28, 32, 119 & 127; Tim Clancy, all others.

Send your thoughts to
books@thomascook.com

- **Found a great bar, club, shop or must-see sight that we don't feature?**
- **Like to tip us off about any information that needs a little updating?**
- **Want to tell us what you love about this handy little guidebook and more importantly how we can make it even handier?**

Then here's your chance to tell all! Send us ideas, discoveries and recommendations today and then look out for your valuable input in the next edition of this title.

Email the above address (stating the title) or write to:
CitySpots Series Editor, Thomas Cook Publishing, PO Box 227, Coningsby Road, Peterborough PE3 8SB, UK.